EFFECTIVE EMAILS

The Secret to Straightforward Communication at Work

CHRIS FENNING

Editing by The Pro Book Editor
Cover Design by Alfie™

eBook ISBN: 978-1-8382440-8-8
paperback ISBN: 978-1-8382440-6-4
hardcover ISBN: 978-1-8382440-7-1
audiobook ISBN: 978-1-8382440-9-5

First Edition

BISAC
BUSINESS & ECONOMICS / Business Communication / General
BUSINESS & ECONOMICS / Business Writing
BUSINESS & ECONOMICS / Skills

This book is dedicated to you.

*You want to write better emails at work
and it's my pleasure to help you achieve that goal.*

CONTENTS

Your free book is waiting

Whether you are heading towards senior leadership, are in the middle of your career, or are a recent graduate, this workbook will help you build the critical skill of clear and concise communication at work

Get a free copy of *The First Minute Workbook* here:
https://chrisfenning.com/get-the-first-minute-workbook-free/
(normally $30)

INTRODUCTION

Email is a major part of how we communicate at work. It can also be the cause of great frustration. How does it feel when people don't read your emails? What about when they only answer one of the multiple questions you asked? If you're anything like me, it is rather annoying.

We are expected to use email effectively from the beginning of our careers, but we are never taught how. There certainly weren't any email writing courses at my school or university. And this lack of training became apparent early in my career. My managers would regularly say, "Chris, your emails are too long. You need to get to the point faster." And they were right, I was cramming all kinds of information into my messages and often putting the most important questions at the end. That meant people didn't read my emails. Or if they did, they only replied to the first question and not the ones farther down.

That feedback set me on a path to learn how to make my emails shorter and clearer. In the beginning, I'd just blamed other people for not replying, or only answering one of the three questions I had asked. It is easy to blame other people, to first wonder why they can't make more effort. But over time I learned that the quality of the replies I received was directly impacted by the quality of the emails I sent. The more I improved my emails, the better the replies became.

At peak times in my career, I sent and received hundreds of emails every day. If the quality of the messages wasn't good, I would waste hours chasing people for replies or trying to make sense of long email chains. The only way I could cope with such a high volume was to increase the quality of every email I sent. The result was an improvement in the quality of the replies I received.

The methods I learned and came to use quite successfully are presented in this book, so you too can learn the wealth of practical advice needed to write shorter, better emails. The techniques you'll learn are based on the following core principles:

- We should send as few emails as possible.
- Emails should be short and easy to understand.
- The way you write emails impacts the quality of the replies you get.

You'll learn the secret to straightforward communication at work, including how to write emails that are short, get to the point, and get better replies. You'll see the positive effect of simple formatting and learn how to avoid frustration in group emails and email chains. By the end of this book, you'll have everything you need to convert email from a frustrating tool into an effective and efficient communication channel for your work.

In **section one,** you'll see why the subject line and introduction to an email are important. The better your introduction, the shorter and clearer the email can be, which in turn leads to higher quality replies.

Section two focuses on layout and formatting. These have a significant impact on how well people read and understand the information, determining whether the reader sees or misses the key information you want to communicate.

Section three looks at group emails, email chains, and what to do when forwarding messages to new people. These often cause confusion, take a lot of time, and cause frustration among groups receiving emails. By the end of this section, you'll know how to handle these emails in a way that is clear, concise, and efficient for everybody involved.

The **final section** includes odd topics that don't fit into the previous three sections, including writing in a non-native language, handling negative exchanges and debates, how to know if you send too many emails, and a final word about how utterly unimportant email sign offs are.

This isn't a theoretical book—it is a practical book. Every section has activities and assessments to help you apply the methods to your own emails. You'll be able to use examples from your work emails to test your skills and practice the methods.

In addition to the lessons, there are activities and assessments to help you test how well you're using these techniques in your emails today and apply the methods to your future emails. And we'll also start working with a really bad email and then apply the advice through the chapters to transform that email into a much more successful communication.

If you're ready to write effective emails, turn the page and we can get started.

HOW TO USE THIS BOOK

We all read and learn in different ways, so I can't tell you there is a right or wrong way to use this book. To fit with as many styles as possible, I've written it to be used in the following ways.

1. **Focus on the key takeaways**. You don't have to search for them. All the key takeaways, advice, and rules are summarized at the beginning of each section and these summaries are also available as free, printable downloads here: https://chrisfenning.com/resources/

2. **Read cover to cover**. If you are brand new to the world of work email, I suggest working through the content in the order it's written. This approach will empower you to form good habits from the start so you can really hit the ground running, without having to figure it all out the hard way or change bad habits later.

3. **Dip in and out**. If you are familiar with sending emails at work and have specific areas you want to improve, you can jump to the topics you are most interested in.

4. **Treat it like a training course.** Instead of reading this like a book, cover to cover, treat it more like a self-paced training course. Work through the sections in order over a period of time, completing the activities and applying the methods to your work emails as you progress through the book.

5. Finally, **this book is a reference guide**. You may want to keep it handy on your desk to help when you're writing a particularly important message and/or less common email activities in your work routines.

EFFECTIVE EMAILS

SECTION 1:
THE FIRST FEW LINES

KEY POINTS

The chances of your email being opened, read, and understood are significantly affected by the subject line and introduction. Follow these methods and your emails will be better than most of the others in your recipient's inbox.

SUBJECT LINE

- Shorter is better.
- Include the topic and purpose.
- Show urgency (if appropriate).
- Avoid false urgency, clickbait, or bait and switch.
- (*if multiple topics*) summarize the common theme or purpose.

TWO FORMULAS FOR CLEAR SUBJECT LINES

- Single-topic emails = [URGENCY] + [TOPIC] + [PURPOSE]

- Multi-topic emails = [URGENCY] + [THEME] + [TOPIC & PURPOSE SUMMARY]

GREETINGS

They are not as important as you think. Observe what people around you use and choose what fits with the culture and what's comfortable for you.

INTRODUCTIONS AND THE FIRST FEW LINES

- Include these four key ingredients in your introduction:
  1. What the email is about.
  2. What the reader must do with it.
  3. What the key message (headline) is.
  4. The expected time frames for any actions are.
- Say how many questions you've asked.
- *If multiple topics*, give a one-line summary of how many topics are in the email, then include all the information in the bullets above.

REPLIES VS. FIRST MESSAGES

Replies do not need to follow the same rules given above for subject lines and introductions. But there are two new rules to use when replying.

1. Don't change the subject line (unless it is inaccurate).
2. Don't say "Thank you" at the start of the reply.

THE STRUCTURE FOR A GOOD INTRODUCTION

[GREETING]

[TOPIC] + [WHAT YOU WANT THE READER TO DO] + [URGENCY] + [KEY MESSAGE] + [TIME FRAMES]

(If appropriate) [NUMBER OF QUESTIONS]
(If appropriate) [LIST THE QUESTIONS]

CASE STUDY: SAM'S EMAIL TO DIANE

Throughout the book, you'll see plenty of examples showing how each technique improves the clarity of an email, and we'll use this case study to work the step-by-step transformation of a difficult-to-read email into a great email as the methods are applied to it. This isn't the only example used in the book, but I want to show you at least one example all the way through so that by the end of section two, you'll see a fully transformed message. Instead of repeating the entire message in each section, the examples may only show pieces of the email to demonstrate a particular method.

Here is the original "poor quality" version of the email before any improvements have been made.

To	Diane@greatplacetowork.com
Subject	FW: FW: FW: RE: Ticket 87D55X

Hi Diane,
We've had calls and some emails from the product and customer service teams. They have a problem with some customers calling and messaging. Apparently there is a problem with the website and the login screen isn't working. I'm not sure exactly what it is because our team hasn't had time to look into the issue yet, but I expect it will take us most of the week to analyze and fix it. We are fully booked for the rest of the month with all the new functionality you requested for the website.
Anyway, the product team wants us to look into the customer website issue, and they want us to do it today. I've included their messages in the email chain below. The full details of the login issue are in customer ticket #87D55X if you want to see the full detail. We are supposed to be supporting them, but, as I said, we are fully booked already. This is a problem for us, we can't do both things. That's why I'm writing to you, to ask for your help. I want to stop some of the work we had planned to

give us time to look at the website issue. I think we can stop one of the three things we are working on, that should give us enough time. The problem is I don't know what work to stop. You are the owner of the website upgrade and so I thought you could help me choose what to stop. Do you have a preference for what we keep working on and what we stop working on? We could stop any of these things: The layout changes for the sidebar menus on the home page. The automation for the PDF generation of customer bills. Or the ask a question form you wanted to add to the contact page. Which one can we stop working on? Does it matter? Or can I just make the choice myself. Apparently this is urgent and the product team wants us to look at it right away. If you can give me your answer in the next hour that would be great. Thank you.

Regards,

Sam

EFFECTIVE EMAILS

INTRODUCTION

The first few lines of an email are so important because they make the email clear and concise, improving the chances that people will reply. In this section, you'll also learn the difference between the first email you send versus dealing with replies and we'll look at how to introduce multiple topics in one email, like when you've got multiple questions, to learn how to do that clearly and concisely.

Finally, there are activities and assessments to test how well you're using these techniques in your emails today and help you apply the methods to your future emails.

GREETINGS - THEY AREN'T AS IMPORTANT AS YOU THINK.

Other books about emails typically include advice on the type of greeting to use in an email. There are pages and pages written about the use of "Hey" instead of "Hello," whether "Dear so-and-so" is too formal, and if you should use first names when you haven't met the person. But I'm not giving you any advice about the specific greetings you should or shouldn't use.

Why not? Because I don't believe there are any universal rules for the right or wrong greeting to use in the variety of situations you'll experience. The appropriateness of a greeting changes depending on your culture, the company culture where you work, how well you know the person you're emailing, the formality of the message, what the people around you use, and much, much more. Not only that, but specific greetings go in and out of fashion over the years. You need to work out what greeting is best based on the situation you are in and be flexible in changing that to the next right approach as things change over time.

If you're really unsure what to use, look at the greetings people send you or ask a friend or manager. Are your colleagues formal or not? Are customer emails started in the same way as internal emails? A quick look at other emails in your company will give you much better guidance than I can.

And finally, the greeting you use is far less important than the quality and clarity of the rest of the email. If you write clear, concise messages, people will care a lot less about whether you said "Hi" or "Hello."

So, with that out of the way, let's look at the first truly important part of an email—the subject line.

SUBJECT LINES SHOULD BE INFORMATIVE

Most of us have inboxes full of emails and every time we look at our inbox, we must choose which message to open first. There are many ways people organize and order their emails—by date, subject, sender, and more—but most people choose which message to open based on two things:

1. Who sent the email; and/or
2. The subject line.

Seeing certain names can prompt us to prioritize opening a message first. It might be your manager, an important client, or the name of someone you've been waiting to get an important message from. Whatever the criteria, the name of the person sending the email influences whether you open it now or wait until later.

This isn't something we can control. When we send an email to someone, we don't define the importance of our name. It doesn't matter how important I think I am, if the other person doesn't share that opinion, I have to accept that they may read a message from someone else first. Luckily, our name isn't the only thing that influences which email people open first. The subject line plays a big part in the decision, and that is something we *can* control.

If a subject line isn't clear and doesn't convey the right level of urgency, it's not going to get people's attention. Knowing the subject line is important is not the same as knowing what to write in the subject line so it will be eye-catching and quickly seen as important by the recipient.

So, what should you write? When it comes to writing an eye catching, informative subject line, what are the right things to include?

The two things that must be in that subject line are the topic and purpose of your communication. In addition, you may highlight the urgency, confidentiality, or other important characteristics of the message if needed.

Topic

If you're sending the first email to someone as opposed to writing a reply, your email is the start of a conversation, so the first thing you should do is let them know what that conversation is about. This is the topic, and it must be clear. If I can't tell what the topic of an email is, I'm not going to know how to prioritize reading it against other things I've been sent.

We all have different priorities, and they change throughout the day. If I'm waiting for a client to send me their questions about a possible sale, I am likely to open their email as soon as I see it in my inbox. While I'm scanning my inbox to determine what to read, the topics in the subject line are assessed against whatever my priority is at that moment. Any email without a clear topic won't capture my attention and thus be less likely to get opened.

What are examples of topics you might use in the subject line? Within a couple of words, you can name the piece of work, the project or the program, or the situation that you want to write about. If you want to write about next month's budget reports, the subject line should include the words, "Next month's budget report," to make it instantly obvious to the recipient what the email is about. If you want to communicate about a particular project (e.g., Project Everest) you could write "Project Everest" in the subject line.

Whatever your topic is, include it in the subject line as a short statement because it only takes a couple of words to make clear what the topic is. Being too wordy here can have the opposite effect.

Purpose

When you send an email, it's because you want the recipient to do something with the information. The topic by itself isn't enough, it doesn't tell the recipient what they need to *do* with the email. Do they need to read and reply to it now, or is the information not needed until next month?

If the receipt doesn't know what they're meant to do with a message, they can't assess how important it is or how time-sensitive it is to prioritize properly. The purpose is what you want the recipient to do with the information you're sending them. Are you asking for help? Need a decision? Giving them an instruction? Are you answering a question they want to know the answer to? Giving someone a heads up about something? The list goes on, but you get the point.

Combining the topic and purpose in the subject line creates a clear statement of what the email is about. Whoever receives your email will understand it and can evaluate whether they should open and read the message, and you've effectively reduced the chances that your message won't be opened/read or prioritized appropriately.

Here's an example.

Next month's budget reports - Hi Sarah, It's that time again, ca...

Figure 1: An ambiguous subject line without clear purpose

The topic of this email is clear, but what is the recipient, Sarah, expected to do with it? Is the purpose to read and understand the information? Does she need to do something? Perhaps Sarah knows what this is for, but as the sender of an email, we should never assume that's the case. Getting the results our emails seek to accomplish is our responsibility.

Without the purpose, the email subject isn't clear. A better version of the subject line is "Next month's budget reports – Need your data by Thursday." This one line makes it clear what the message is about and what the recipient is being asked to do. Even better, there is also a clear time frame for the response that will help the recipient prioritize the message against the other emails in their inbox.

It only takes a few words to make the purpose clear. Here are some more examples of subject lines that include the purpose for the budget report email.

- Next month's budget report: Send me your questions
- Next month's budget report: Need your information by Monday (7/8)
- Next month's budget report: Please approve your unit's numbers
- Next month's budget report: The data you requested is attached

Each of these subjects has a clear topic and purpose, so the recipient will know what the email is about and what they are expected to do with it. When the information is this clear, you increase the chances of people reading and following through on your emails.

Short Subject Lines Are Better

An effective subject line doesn't need to be long. In fact, it should be short. The fewer words it takes to convey the topic and purpose, the better. Not only are short subjects quicker to read but they are also more likely to be displayed to the recipient. Many emails are read on tablets or phones, and devices with small screens often cut the subject lines short. The shorter you keep your subject line, the greater the chance it'll fit on the screen.

> **Next budget report: Need your info by Mon-7th** - Hi Sarah, Ca...
>
> **Next month's budget report: Need your information by Mond...**

Figure 2: Long subject lines are often truncated. Shorter versions are more likely to be displayed in full

Here are a few ways to shorten the budget report examples.

- Feb budget report: Send me your questions
- Sept budget report: Need your info by 16-Aug
- Dec budget report: Pls approve your numbers
- Sept budget report: Your data is attached

Exactly how you shorten the subject will vary. Your communication style, the company policy, and the formality of the message should all play a part. When sending a contract to a major client, a subject line of "Annual retainer contract – request for signature" is probably more appropriate than "contract – pls sign now," for example. Use your judgment for what is appropriate, and if in doubt, look at what other people around you are doing and ask a colleague or your boss.

CASE STUDY: Improving Sam's Email to Diane

To	Diane@greatplacetowork.com
Subject	FW: FW: FW: RE: Ticket 87D55X

Hi Diane,

We've had calls and some emails from the product and customer service teams...

The subject line indicates the topic is ticket number 87D55X. But after reading the email, we discover the ticket refers to a problem with the website. The ticket may be the cause of Sam's message to Diane, but it is not the topic of this email. The main topic is the need to choose a website upgrade to stop. This can be shortened to "Website upgrades," and will likely be more meaningful to Diane than a ticket number.

Clarifying the topic is helpful, but it doesn't tell Diane why she should open and read the message. We know the purpose is to get Diane's help choosing an upgrade to stop work on. Adding this purpose to the subject line makes it much clearer what the email is about.

To	Diane@greatplacetowork.com
Subject	Website upgrades – Need help choosing one to stop

Hi Diane,

We've had calls and some emails from the product and customer service teams...

Handling Multiple Topics

As you've no doubt experienced, emails often include more than one topic. The principles for writing a clear subject line for a multi-topic email are largely the same as those used for single-topic emails. The main difference is that the application of those principles becomes harder.

The more topics you have in your email, the harder it becomes to write a clear, informative, and relevant subject line and to make it short in the interest of increasing how much is viewable on smaller screens.

With more than one topic in the email, you want to keep to the principles of a good subject line shown so far but need to include each topic and its purpose, like this:

One topic subject line	TOPIC + PURPOSE
Two topic subject line	TOPIC 1 + PURPOSE 1 + TOPIC 2 + PURPOSE 2
Three topic subject line	TOPIC 1 + PURPOSE 1 + TOPIC 2 + PURPOSE 2 + TOPIC + PURPOSE 3

As you can see, the subject lines get longer with the addition of each new topic. The longer the subject line, the more likely it is to be cut short when viewed on a phone or tablet. Plus, the recipient may only read the first topic before deciding whether to open the email. Both of these make multi-topic subject lines less effective.

Fortunately, there are ways to shorten the subject lines and still keep them clear. (Note: Deciding whether to send multiple emails instead of combining them will be discussed later.) The solution is to summarize the topics and purposes. If two topics share a common theme, the theme can be used in the subject line. Likewise, if separate topics have a similar purpose, include a joint purpose in the subject line.

Topics With a Common Theme

If the topics in an email share a common theme, the subject line should start with the common theme. This tells the reader that everything in the email is related to the same thing. The rest of the subject line should summarize the topics and purposes as briefly as possible.

Here are some examples:

- Feb sales report – Status update & audit questions
- Jefferson account – Contract language & project dates you asked for
- Vacation handover – Project info & tasks for you
- Office supplies – Send me your orders & see new process info

In each case, the first words before the dash name the common theme and the rest of the subject line shows the different topics and purposes. Be aware: if there are more than two topics, you'll need to summarize them together. Modifying the examples above to include three or more topics could look like this:

- Vacation handover – Everything you need to know & do
- Jefferson Account – Multiple updates & actions
- Office supplies – Read & follow if you want your supplies

The format used in these examples is:

(THEME) + (TOPIC & PURPOSE SUMMARY)

In each example, the topics and purposes are clear even though the subject line is less specific. The person receiving the email will know enough to choose whether to open it (or not!) and how to prioritize it more in line with meeting your and their responsibilities.

Different Topics With a Common Purpose

Similar to the method described above, you can combine common purposes even if the topics don't share a common theme. For example:

- Project ABC updates & new vacation policy – please share with your team
- Status update for Projects ABC & XYZ – please read and send questions
- Things to complete before you go on vacation

The common purpose in each of these examples makes it reasonable to combine the topics into one message.

No Common Topics or Purpose

If the topics and purposes do not share any common themes, you should write separate emails for each topic to increase the chance that you'll get a reply to each topic. It also slows down replies to combine too many things in one email, because people wait until they have answers to all the topics before replying to your message. Plus, and this may be minor or significant depending on how you manage your email, emails with two or more unrelated topics are frustrating to file and organize. They either end up with multiple labels or, in some cases, the message is duplicated and each copy is saved to a different topic folder. That issue continues with every reply in the ensuing chain too.

I can't give you a number for how many topics are too many for a single email. There are some situations where it makes sense to include a lot of topics in a single message. For example, if you are writing a vacation handover message where you include information about separate pieces of work, which works because there is a common theme of "Vacation handing over."

While there isn't a strict rule for the number of topics, there is a rule for the number of themes to include, and one theme per email is best. The theme can contain multiple topics if they relate to the theme.

The only exception is to allow two themes if there is a single clear purpose, such as passing information on to other people. (e.g., Project ABC updates & new vacation policy – please share with your team). Even though this technically works, it is usually better to split the different themes into separate emails to make it easier to manage and organize replies.

To make the information above clearer, here is a simple diagram to help you choose how many emails to write.

	Multiple purposes	One purpose
One theme	One email is usually fine *	One email is fine
Multiple themes	Write separate emails	Separate emails are usually better *

Figure 3: Choose how many emails to write using this theme/purpose grid

* In both cases a single email is fine if the topics are small (i.e., quick to describe and of low consequence) and the purpose is simple for the recipient to understand and complete. If the topics are large, complex, have high impact, and/or the purpose of the message is complex, write multiple emails.

In all four of these situations, the subject line should make it clear what topic(s) are in the email.

When Not to Send a Separate Email for Each Topic

If it's so important to keep topics separate, wouldn't it be simpler to limit each email to just one topic?

Yes and no. If each email includes a single topic, it would be clear what the email is about, but there are a few reasons why this isn't the best advice universally.

First, we don't naturally communicate about one topic at a time. It is human nature to group similar topics together when talking and writing. Instead of trying to change this ingrained style, it's actually simpler to learn to organize a message to keep topics separate.

Second, when multiple topics relate to each other, it can be more efficient to think about and respond to them all at the same time. Studies have shown that our brains aren't efficient if we have to repeatedly switch context. Every time we change tasks, it takes time to get our thoughts in order and focus on the new task.[1] Sending multiple emails causes the recipient to assess the context for each one separately, even if they are related. Think about it this way, would you prefer to receive one email with five tasks on the same theme, or five separate emails each with a separate task? Most people prefer to have the related tasks and activities listed in one email. Combining topics with a similar theme into one email helps the recipient focus on the singular context of the theme, which in turn makes it easier to read, react, and respond to the different topics.

The final reason not to limit emails to one topic each is that this would increase the number of emails we send and receive. I don't know about you, but I get enough emails already. The thought of doubling or tripling that number fills me with dread. I'd rather have a smaller number of well-organized messages than a string of separate messages on related topics.

If you're unsure if the topics in your email relate to a common theme, try this simple activity:

Imagine you phoned someone to talk about the topics in your email. You talk about the first topic, then hang up. An hour later, you call the same person and talk about the second topic. How likely is it the other person will think or say, "Why didn't you talk about this in the first phone call?" If the chances are high that they would think this, the topics share a common theme and you can write one email with them both. Anytime topics feel like they should be separate phone calls, write them as separate emails.

Conveying Urgency

If you want to show a message is urgent, there are features in most email applications that enable this, like setting the priority to high, flagging, and adding a timed reply-notification. In addition to, or instead of, these features, the subject line can indicate the urgency of the message.

Adding [URGENT] at the start of a subject line makes the email stand out in any inbox. Urgent messages are likely to get attention, and likewise, putting [Not urgent] helps the recipient see they don't need to read it right away. They might still open it if your name is high on their priority list, but that's up to them. At least you've let them know something isn't urgent.

Whatever method you choose, you don't need to indicate the level of urgency in every email. Only use priority indicators when a message needs to stand out or overuse will quickly make this no longer work for you.

There are many ways to indicate urgency. Here are some examples:

- URGENT
- PLEASE READ
- REPLY NEEDED BY 10AM
- IMPORTANT
- MUST READ

The use of capital letters isn't required but helps the message stand out in the list of emails only showing sender and subject line information. It may also help to put the words in brackets to further separate the urgency indicator from the rest of the subject line. Here are some examples.

- [URGENT] Dec budget report: Pls approve your numbers
- [REPLY NEEDED BY 10AM] Dec budget report: Pls approve your numbers
- [low priority] Sept budget report: Need your info by 16-Aug

Always put the priority at the start of the subject line. If you put it at the end, it may be cut off if the subject line is truncated in the email application.

Here's what an inbox looks like when the priority is clearly stated in the subject line. How easy is it to spot the important message?

Next budget report: Need your info by Mon-7th - Hi Sarah, Ca...

Next month's budget report: Need your information by Mond...

[URGENT] Sept budget report: Need your info by 16-Aug - Hi ...

FW: FW: FW: FW: Re: FYI - 3G587P92 - Hi Sarah, It's that time a...

Sept budget report: Need your info by 16-Aug - Hi Sarah, It's t...

Next month's budget report: Read and send me your questio...

Next month's budget reports - Hi Sarah, It's that time again, ca...

Figure 4: Urgent messages stand out when the priority is at the start of the subject line

WARNING: Be careful when using this approach. Overusing the [URGENT] can stop it from being effective. It's a bit like the boy who cried wolf, and you will probably get fewer responses overall because people will get frustrated and treat your messages as decidedly *un*-urgent.

If something is really urgent, you should consider a different method of communication. You can send the detail or data by email and then contact the person to discuss it. Phone, instant message, or going to see the person are all better ways to communicate when you need a quick reply.

Using labels in the subject line isn't limited to showing urgency. Anytime you want the recipients to treat a message in a specific way, you can put a label in the subject line. Examples of labels you may use are:

- [CONFIDENTIAL]
- [DO NOT SHARE]

These labels follow the same principles as defining urgency.

CASE STUDY: Improving Sam's Email to Diane

The email to Diane doesn't include any sense of urgency. The content of the email tells us Sam needs a decision quickly, so the team doesn't stop working on the wrong upgrade.

We can continue the improvement of the example subject line by adding an urgency label:

To	Diane@greatplacetowork.com
Subject	[URGENT] Website upgrades – Need help choosing one to stop

Information-Only Messages

I'm often asked, "What about information-only emails? They don't need any action. Can I put FYI in the subject line instead of the purpose?"

My response is always the same, that there is no such thing as an information-only message.

Saying a message is "information only" implies no action is needed. But there is no such thing as an email that doesn't require *any* action at all. At the very least, you want people to read the message. That is an action. Beyond that slightly pedantic answer, there is always something you want people to do with the information. Otherwise, why would you share it?

One reason people—especially managers—send information-only messages is because they want the recipients to read the content and identify how the information impacts them or their work. We don't always know how information will impact other people. So instead of guessing, or assuming, share it and let them work out the impact for themselves. Then they can take appropriate action. If there is an impact, the recipient should take appropriate action. That could be asking follow-up questions, making a change of some kind to their work, adding a risk to a risk management plan on a project, or any one of countless other actions.

As for writing "FYI" in the subject line, no, you should not do that. FYI isn't a clear purpose, and without a clear purpose, you reduce the chances that people will read the email as we learned earlier.

If you find yourself about to send an information-only message, stop and take ten seconds to write a subject line with a clear purpose. Something like "Please review and identify if this impacts you" is sufficient. If you want to keep the subject line really short, you can say "TOPIC + Please review for impacts" to tell the recipient they need to read the email and determine if they must take any action.

Avoid These Three Types of Subject Line

The goal of any subject line is to get the recipient to open and read your email in the appropriate time frame. But if taken too far, the goal of getting people to open your messages can have the opposite effect. To avoid this problem, there are three things you mustn't use in your work email subject lines:

- False urgency;
- Clickbait; and/or
- Bait and switch.

These three methods are often used in marketing or sales emails, and I bet you've got a few of them in your inbox right now. These methods are also common in adverts and blog post titles. The purpose of these methods is to increase the chance you'll open a message (or click on a link) to find out more. While you do want to increase the chances that people will read your work emails, using any of these three methods will damage your reputation. And, in the long run, people will start ignoring your messages or leaving them until later, because they don't trust what you write in your subject line.

False Urgency

Overusing urgency labels can stop them from being effective. Use these labels sparingly and only if absolutely necessary. It's a bit like the boy who cried wolf—if you label every email as urgent when it isn't, people will stop treating them as urgent. That means the really urgent messages will be lost among all the others you've sent. Not only that but you will probably get fewer responses overall because people will get frustrated and treat your all of your messages as decidedly un-urgent.

Clickbait

Clickbait subject lines are the go-to method for email marketing and sales messages. I bet if you check your personal email account right now, you'll see subject lines like: "Have you heard about the next big thing yet?" or "Don't miss this great deal! Only one more day!"

Clickbait is designed to attract attention and is a good way to encourage people to open a message. One definition of clickbait defines the approach as, "Something designed to make readers want to click on a link that leads to content of dubious value or interest." [2]

Other sources say clickbait adds an element of dishonesty, using enticements that do not accurately reflect the content being delivered. [3]

The fact that the definitions of clickbait include "dubious value or interest" and "elements of dishonesty" should be enough to persuade you not to use these in your emails at work. Then again, perhaps we'd have more success with people reading our status updates if they started with, "5 project updates you won't believe have happened!" *(That was a joke, but if you try it and it works without undesirable consequences, let me know. I'll add it to the next version of this book!)*

An example of a clickbait subject line is, "Critical project update – please read," and the email is then about a minor typo update in a non-critical project document. While I am strongly in favor of correct spellings, even I wouldn't list a typo change as a critical update.

There is a big difference between making a subject line enticing (clickbait) and making it informative and useful. The latter is far more appropriate for workplace emails. Leave the enticing subject lines to the email marketing teams and stick with informative and useful.

Bait and Switch

Merriam-Webster dictionary defines bait and switch as offering a person something desirable to gain their interest then giving them something less desirable.[4]

When the subject doesn't match the content of the message, this is bait and switch. It differs from clickbait because while clickbait falsely indicates the importance or value of the email content, bait and switch messages have little to no relationship between the subject and the content.

Imagine how you'd feel if you got a message like this:

Subject	Extra vacation day this year
Hi Josh, HR has sent out the new vacation allowance and it includes an extra day. Speaking of vacation, I need you to work next weekend because we are short-staffed.	

The subject line promises something great—an extra vacation day—but the email is really about working extra shifts. How many emails like this do you think you can send before people will distrust you or stop opening your messages? Probably not very many.

The Formula for a Great Subject Line

To recap the important points we've covered so far: An email's subject line influences the chances of it being opened and getting the attention it needs. We can't control the order in which people read their emails, but a good subject line can increase the chances that our messages will be opened and not ignored.

Two formulas for clear subject lines:

- Single-topic emails = [URGENCY] + [TOPIC] + [PURPOSE]
- Multi-topic emails = [URGENCY] + [THEME] + [TOPIC & PURPOSE SUMMARY]

Email subject lines that use these structures give the recipient all they need to make an informed choice about when to open the message.

In addition to using the formula, make sure to only use urgency labels when absolutely necessary and don't write clickbait or bait and switch subject lines.

Here are a few more examples of less-than-ideal subject lines along with better versions using the methods described in this section:

- **Bad:** Here you go
- **Better:** April sales numbers – please update the reports
- **Format:** TOPIC + PURPOSE

- **Bad:** URGENT!!!
- **Better:** [URGENT] Check if this announcement impacts Projects Apex & Everest
- **Format:** URGENCY + PURPOSE + TOPICS

- **Bad:** FW: FW: FW: RE: FW: FW: Derek
- **Better:** Derek is leaving – Please share gift ideas
- **Format:** TOPIC + PURPOSE

- **Bad:** Status update
- **Better:** Project Apex – status is yellow – need help with three items
- **Format:** THEME + (TOPIC & PURPOSE SUMMARY)

- **Bad:** FYI
- **Better:** Resource changes – should I be worried?
- **Format:** TOPIC + PURPOSE

- **Bad:** New priorities??
- **Better:** Re. CEO priorities statement – does it impact us?
- **Format:** TOPIC + PURPOSE

- **Bad:** FW: FW: FW: FW: Re: FYI - 3G587P92
- **Better:** Please update case file #3G587P92 today
- **Format:** PURPOSE + TOPIC + URGENCY

In these examples, you can see the topic and purpose can switch places. This sometimes happens from a combination of the way we structure sentences and our personal styles. Generally, it is better to have the topic before the purpose, but they can switch places if the subject line is short enough.

And finally, never send an email with a blank subject line. This may seem obvious, but it happens more than you think. A blank subject line is a great way to ensure people will ignore your message while providing them with the excuse that they didn't see it.

INTRODUCE YOUR EMAIL CLEARLY

The first few lines of an email are like the start of a conversation. As described in my previous book, *The First Minute*[5], the start of a conversation prepares the recipient to understand and interpret everything else you will share. It's no different when writing an email. The first few lines are the introduction that sets up everything else in the message.

Why does an email need an introduction? A good introduction increases the chances your email will be read, understood, and replied to. A bad introduction causes confusion and frustration and lowers the chance of getting a complete response.

When most people read an email, they read the first line and then scan the rest of the message to find important information. They're going to read the first line, but there's no guarantee they'll read everything in the rest of the message. Therefore, you want the first line to be as efficient and effective as possible. It must convey the critical information you need the recipient to have and help them understand what else is contained in the email.

To do this, there are three rules to follow:

1. Include the four key ingredients of a good introduction;
2. State the number of questions asked in the email; and
3. Introduce multiple topics (if more than one topic).

The Four Key Ingredients of a Good Introduction

These four things included in the first lines can make your emails clear and give your email the best chance of being fully read and understood:

1. What it is about;
2. What the reader must do;
3. The key message; and
4. Time frames.

These four things show what the email is about, what the re̲.̲.̲.̲ must do with the information, and when a response or action is expected. This information should be the first thing the recipient reads and take no more than one hundred words (five sentences) to convey, so they will quickly see it without having to hunt for it and know when a response or action is needed.

Time frames shouldn't just be about specific and urgent deadlines. They are also needed to show when things don't need to be rushed. In fact, studies in 2021 show the importance of stating when a message is not important. People receiving emails overestimate the urgency of a response by 36 percent[6] and also experience increased levels of stress. To avoid causing your recipients unintended stress, include a line like, "This is not an urgent matter so you can get to it whenever you can." This one line can totally remove the stress and false sense of urgency the recipient might feel.

You may have noticed that the introduction and the subject line include similar information, and this is intentional. After all, if the subject line didn't match the content of the email, it wouldn't be a good subject line. The repetition of topic and purpose ensures the recipient better understands the message.

Sometimes the four key ingredients are enough for the entire email. In this case, the introduction becomes the complete message and you don't need to write anything else except a sign off. This usually happens when a topic is small, simple to describe, or doesn't need a lot of extra information. When you start using this introduction, you might find some of your emails get shorter, taking less of your time.

CASE STUDY: Improving Sam's Email to Diane

Looking at the website decision email to Diane, how many of the four elements can you see in the introduction? To make it simpler (and to save space on the page!) I've included only the first few lines from the original email.

To	Diane@greatplacetowork.com
Subject	FW: FW: FW: RE: Ticket 87D55X

Hi Diane,

We've had calls and some emails from the product and customer service teams. They have a problem with some customers calling and messaging. Apparently there is a problem with the website and the login screen isn't working. I'm not sure exactly what it is because our team hasn't had time to look into the issue yet but I expect it will take us most of the week to analyze and fix it. We are fully booked for the rest of the month with all the new functionality you requested for the website. Anyway, the product team wants us to look into the customer website issue, and they want us to do it today.

From this introduction can you tell what the email is about?

When I read it, these are the topics I see introduced in the first few lines:

1. A problem the customer service team is having;
2. The website login page isn't working;
3. The team doesn't have time to investigate;
4. The team is booked up all month; and
5. The product team wants the issue investigated today.

In the first 115 words, Sam (the sender of the email) has introduced five topics. What isn't clear is which topic, or theme, is the focus of the email. The rest of the email could be about any of these topics. And yet it isn't. If you read the full email earlier in the book, you will have seen the main topic is the website upgrade work the IT team is doing for Diane.

Not only is the main topic not clear, but it also isn't clear what Diane is supposed to do with the information in the email.

It doesn't mention the decision for which website upgrade to stop or that Diane needs to be part of that decision.

The key message isn't clear either, and it also has no time frame. In fact, the original introduction is missing all four of the important pieces of information.

Here is a revised introduction to the email, applying the four elements. Not only is this message clearer, but it is also shorter, having ninety-two words compared to the original 115.

To	Diane@greatplacetowork.com
Subject	[URGENT] Website upgrades – Need help choosing one to stop

Hi Diane,

We need to stop work on one website upgrades planned for this month and would like your help choosing which upgrade to stop. There is an urgent customer login issue on the website that our team must fix this week – we only heard about it this morning. The situation and the decision to make are described below.

Question: Can you let us know the upgrade we should stop before 11am today?

I'll also call you to discuss this, but wanted you to have the info in writing to read first.

The revised introduction includes all four pieces of information for a great introduction. The first line of the message gets straight to the point. After reading the first twenty-five words, Diane will know what the message is about and what Sam is asking her to do. The key information about the situation is given next, and the most important question for Diane to answer is clearly labeled. There is also a clearly stated time frame for Diane to reply. By including the four pieces of key information in the first few lines,

Diane is prepared to read the rest of the email. No matter how much information comes next, she knows what it is all about.

NOTE: The revised introduction uses blank space and a bold formatted label for the question. This makes it easier to read and helps Diane see the important question right away. These techniques, along with other types of formatting, are covered in more detail in section two.

Say How Many Questions Are Present

A good introduction also makes clear how many questions are included in the email to increase the chances that all of them get answered. For example, if you're asking three questions, saying you're asking three questions right up front will prepare the recipient to know right from the start that they shouldn't just answer the first question they come across and hit Reply. They are more likely to look for three questions to answer in their reply because they are expecting them.

This information can be given in addition to the four key ingredients you just read about, or it could be part of saying what you'd like the reader to do. For example "I'd like your help to answer three questions about the kick-off for Project Apex."

You may not know how many questions you're going to ask when you start writing the email. Therefore, when you've finished writing, go back and count the number of questions and then add that number to the introduction.

Finally, if your email has a single topic, it can help to list all the questions together as part of or immediately after the introduction. Then, if more information is needed, it can be given in the rest of the email.

For example:

To	Poorna@greatplacetowork.com
Subject	Staff away day – questions about the afternoon agenda

Hi Poorna,

I am finalizing the agenda for Friday's staff away day. Can you help clarify a few things about the afternoon? I have three questions for you, more detail about each question is included later in the email.

1. Do I need to include time for the CEO to give a closing speech?
2. Did the extra budget for the food get approved?
3. Are we sending the full agenda to everyone before the event?

[More info about each question might be written in the rest of the email ...]

NOTE: If you have multiple topics, it may not make sense to group them together. The questions could be spread out through the body of the email as long as the introduction says how many questions there are in total.

Introducing Multi-Topic Emails

If the introduction is important for single-topic emails, it is doubly so for emails with multiple topics. As I mentioned earlier, people often read the first few lines of an email and only scan the rest. They don't read every word in the message. If you don't make it clear there are multiple topics right at the start, the recipient might respond to only the first topic. Sure, it won't happen every time, some people will read the entire email and respond to both topics. But why take the chance? Make it clear there are multiple topics at the start, and you'll increase the odds of getting the complete reply you need.

Drawing a comparison with face-to-face conversation, you might start by saying, "Can I talk to you about a couple of things?" This makes it clear there is more than one topic in the conversation and helps you structure the conversation around those two topics. It's the same when starting an email.

Introducing a multi-topic email follows the previous two rules. It should include the four key ingredients and indicate how many questions there are.

1. What it is about = Say how many topics there are, what the topics are, and if there is a common theme;
2. What the reader must do for each topic;
3. The key message for each topic; and
4. Time frames, either separate for each topic or combined for the overall email.

There are many ways you can structure a multiple-topic introduction, but in all cases, the first sentence should say how many topics there are in the message. After that, you can choose how to structure the information. Some options are to write two separate short paragraphs or a summary that includes both topics. The situation, your own style, and the amount of information you want to include in the overall email will affect which approach is better.

Here's an example:

To	Nidhi@Projectoffice.com
Subject	Project Everest – Questions about Budget and project lead

Hi Nidhi,

Can you help me with a couple of things on Project Everest? The first is a decision about who should lead the project. The second is a question about the project budget deadlines. The questions and more info for each topic are given below. If you can get back to me before the end of Thursday, I'd really appreciate it. Thanks.

Topic 1: Who should lead the project?
Blah blah blah blah blah blah …

Topic 2: Budget deadlines
Blah blah blah blah blah blah …

Thanks,
Paulo

Making it clear there are two topics and what each is named but leaving the detail until later in the message helps Nidhi have a basic idea of all the important points of the email before getting into the detail of either one.

Skip the Introduction if the Topics are Small

If the topics are quick to describe and don't much information, the four key ingredients for each topic might be enough to make up the entire email. In that case, you can introduce the email with a single line saying there are two topics and then write a paragraph for each topic. There's no need to introduce both topics only to then duplicate the info in the rest of the message, making the email longer than needed and wasting time for you and the reader. Use your own judgment to determine when each approach fits the situation best.

WARNING: Whatever you do, do not introduce the email as though it has a single topic and then add a second or third topic part way through the message. This is not quite as bad as a bait and switch email, but it does cause problems. The message as a whole is harder to read because the reader must spend extra effort working out how the various topics relate to each other. It is also much more likely that you'll get an incomplete response if the recipient only replies to the single topic mentioned in the introduction.

Replies are different from the first email

Everything up to this point has been about the first email in a conversation, so we need to take a moment and look at the difference between replies versus the first email. Why? Because what we write in the subject line and introductions of a first email doesn't always apply to replies.

The first email we send is the start of a conversation. It may be written down, but it's the same as walking up to someone or picking up the phone and calling them. You are starting a new exchange of information and should define the topic before you go into detail. Replies, however, already have a defined topic and purpose. When you reply to an email, you don't need to set up your message because you are already in the middle of a conversation. If you were talking to somebody face-to-face or on the phone, you wouldn't introduce the subject and purpose of that conversation every time it's your turn to speak. You wouldn't go through the process of restating the key topic or the time frames or anything else. That would be weird. It doesn't make sense to do that in a conversation, and it doesn't make sense in an email either.

Are there any rules for writing email replies?

Most of the advice in this book applies to the first email in a conversation and also to replies. In a few places I will call out exceptions that are specific to replies, but overall, you can apply the methods in the rest of this book to all the emails you send.

With that said, there are two rules for replies that are specific to the subject line and the introduction:

1. Don't change the subject line.
2. Don't say "Thank you" at the start of a reply.

Don't Change the Subject Line.

Changing the subject line causes problems in tracking and filing emails, especially for anyone who organizes their inbox by conversation. A change in title splits the conversation into two threads/chains, which is a recipe for frustration and not getting replies.

If it's a new subject, start a new email with the new subject line and follow the advice for writing a new email. We'll cover this more in section three when talking about changing topics in an email chain.

There are two exceptions to this rule:

Exception 1:

If the topic in the subject line is inaccurate and that has a real impact on the conversation, then change the subject. For example, if an email topic relates to a numbered or named event, like an order number or a customer service ticket number, and the number is incorrect, it is okay to change it to the correct number, *but* make sure you tell everyone in the email chain what you changed and why. Don't make a change and not announce it. That's a quick way to confuse and frustrate other recipients who may lose track of the conversation in their inboxes.

Exception 2:

If the subject line is full of RE: and FW: tags. Most modern email systems don't include the RE for reply and FW for forward tags, but if you're working on an older system that does automatically add them, it is okay to remove these from the subject line. The email tracking and conversation grouping should still work fine if you tidy these up, and doing so can ensure more of the subject line will be visible in smaller windows/screens.

Don't Say "Thank You" at the Start of a Reply.

Hassan Osman, email expert and author of the great book, *Don't Reply All*, has a tip I'd like to share with you. Hassan suggests you never start an email with the words "Thank you," especially if you have additional questions or information to share in the email. Emails are often squeezed into small spaces on small screens, and if the message preview for your email only shows the first few words of your message, the recipient might only see your "Thank you," assume that was all you had to say, and not open the email. As Hassan says, "They falsely assume that you're just acknowledging their response and they move on." If they don't open the message, they won't see the additional questions or information you shared, which leaves you waiting for a follow-up email that will never arrive.

To avoid this, Hassan suggests typing your follow-up questions before you say thank you for their earlier response. Here's an example:

To	Poorna@greatplacetowork.com
Subject	Re. Project Everest – change in funding status
Hi Poorna, Does this mean we are stopping work immediately on Project Everest? If yes, will you tell the team or should I? Thanks for making the decision, and for the detailed reply to my earlier questions. Chris	

Structuring the reply in this way shows the recipient there is a question to answer and reduces the chance that they skip the email.

In summary, type your follow-up questions and actions first and thank them later.

ASSESSMENT
HOW DO YOU START YOUR EMAILS?

For this self-assessment activity, find the last five emails you sent that started a new conversation or topic. Emails that reply to other people's messages won't work for this assessment. Use those emails to answer the questions below but from the perspective of the recipient. Put yourself in their shoes, on the receiving end, and decide if you gave the best possible clarity using the smallest number of words.

NOTE: Longer emails tend to work better for this activity, but it's okay to use short messages if that's all you have available.

Do the subject lines make the topics clear?	Yes/No/Sometimes
Do the subject lines make it clear why the recipient is getting the email?	Yes/No/Sometimes
Do the first lines of the email contain the topic, the purpose, a summary of the key message, and relevant time frames?	Yes/No/Sometimes
If there are multiple topics, do the subject line and introduction make it clear there are multiple topics in the email?	Yes/No/Sometimes
Do you say how many questions are in the message?	Yes/No/Sometimes
Is the urgency of the message clear to the recipients?	Yes/No/Sometimes

THINGS TO CONSIDER

If you circled YES for each question, well done. You start your emails clearly.

If you circled NO, or SOMETIMES for any (or all) of the questions, don't worry. You're not doing anything bad or wrong, but your email might not be as effective as you want. Consider what changes you can make to improve the brevity and clarity of your message.

What specific parts of your email introductions do you need to improve? What will you do to improve the next emails you send?

_____

_____

_____

_____

_____

_____

_____

You can download a copy of this assessment here:
https://chrisfenning.com/resources/

ACTIVITY
PREPARE YOUR NEXT THREE EMAIL
INTRODUCTIONS

This activity will help you practice the email introduction methods.

Pick three topics you need to send emails for in the next week. These should be new topics for the recipient and not a reply to an existing email. The topics should also be more than a one or two line comment or question. The larger and more complex the topic, the better it is for this activity.

For each topic, write the subject line and first few lines of the email in the spaces below. The subject line and introduction must make the following things clear to the recipient:

- The topic and purpose;
- What they need to do (if anything);
- A summary of the key information; and
- Any time frames they need to know about.

Email Introduction #1:

To	
Subject	

(Don't write the entire email for the purpose of this exercise.)

Email Introduction #2:

To	
Subject	

(Don't write the entire email for the purpose of this exercise.)

Email Introduction #3:

To	
Subject	

(Don't write the entire email for the purpose of this exercise.)

THINGS TO CONSIDER

- Does this approach change how you think about what to write in the rest of the email?
- Did any of the introductions end up being the entire email message?
- Will your emails be shorter if you use this method?
- Does writing an introduction help identify if an email can split into two or more messages?

You can download a copy of this activity here:
https://chrisfenning.com/resources/

SECTION 2:
LENGTH, LAYOUT & FORMATTING

KEY POINTS

The length, layout, and formatting you use can make a world of difference to the clarity of your emails. Short emails are easier to read. The chance of getting a complete reply to your message is higher if you use good structure. Follow these methods and your emails will be better laid out and easier to read than most of the others in your recipient's inbox. At the end of the section, there is an assessment so you can see how well you're applying these to your own emails.

Short Emails Are Better Emails

To make your emails as short as possible, include the following information and nothing more:
- The topic and purpose of the email;
- What specific action or response you want them to do;
- The time frame in which to do it;
- Just enough detail for them to understand the situation and move ahead with whatever they need to do; and/or
- Nothing that gets in the way or confuses the topic or purpose.

White Space, Bullets, Numbered Lists, & Headings

- Longer and/or complex/multi-topic emails need *more* structure.
- Include white space between paragraphs and keep paragraphs short.
- Use text formatting to call attention to key information.
- Put all lists in bullet point format or use a numbered list.
- Numbered lists help people reply faster.
- In long emails, use headings to break up and organize the message.

MAKE ALL QUESTIONS, ACTIONS, & DECISIONS STAND OUT

- Put them on their own lines.
- Label them and use formatting (e.g., bold text).
- In group emails state the name of the person/people it is directed to.
- When replying, repeat questions from other people's emails.

GRAPHICS

Graphics can help convey a message clearly, but they don't always download, open, or display correctly on mobile devices. If you want to use graphics, make sure you:

- Add the image as an attachment instead of embedding it in the email; and
- Only add images if it adds value and strengthens the message.

ATTACHMENTS & HYPERLINKS

Use attachments and links for supplemental details to keep emails short and follow these rules:

- **DO** tell the recipient why there is an attachment.
- **DO** say what's in the attachment.
- **DO** say why they need to read it.
- **DO** name attachments clearly.
- **DON'T** leave key information in the attachment (**DO** add it to the email).
- **DO** use clickable hyperlinks instead of text URL.
- **DO** place the hyperlinks in the relevant places in the body of the email (**DON'T** list them all in one place).

TEMPLATES

When you have a good template, you not only save time creating the emails but it is easier for your audience to receive and understand that information.

A TEMPLATE FOR GOOD STRUCTURE

Combining the rules and advice from section two with the subject line and introduction advice in section one produces a structure template for a good work email. No matter what the topic, the audience, or the industry, using the structure below will produce better emails.

Subject	[URGENCY] + [TOPIC] + [PURPOSE]

[Greeting]

Introduction:
[Topic] + [What you want the reader to do] + [Urgency]
[Key message] + [Time frames] + [Number of questions]
(If appropriate) [List the questions]

Main body of the message:
[White space]
[Bullet points]
[Labels for questions, actions, and decisions]
[Limited text formatting]

If multiple topics: [Separate topics with headers]
If using attachments or links: [Link or attachment] + [Topic + Purpose for the extra information]

End:
[Sign off]

INTRODUCTION

Length, layout, and formatting impact how easy your emails are to read. They change how well people respond to your messages, or if they even respond at all!

In this section, you'll learn why it's almost always better to write shorter emails and what you do and don't need to include to make a message as short as possible.

While the goal is to write as short an email as possible, sometimes they do need to be long. The later parts of this section show how to make longer emails easier to read. You'll discover the effect whitespace, bullets, and numbered lists have on your message, as well as simple ways to make questions, actions, and decisions stand out. All of which help you get answers from the right people.

We'll also take a look at what to do with recurring emails. These are the messages that you're sending on a regular basis, like team updates or status emails. There are some simple things you can do to help make those recurring emails easier for yourself and recipients.

There are activities and assessments included in this section as well to help you apply these methods in your email activities.

SHORT EMAILS ARE BETTER EMAILS

You probably don't need me to tell you this, but people are more likely to read emails that are short. This is because longer emails have more text and longer paragraphs. The denser the text, the harder it is for the recipient to understand. They have to work harder to find the important information and know what they need to do with it.

People are also more likely to reply faster to shorter messages. If you take a moment to think about the way you read emails, I'm willing to bet you read and respond to shorter emails first. I am no different. I have to put more effort into reading a longer email and resist the temptation of leaving it until later.

If you need more evidence that shorter is better when it comes to email length, the experiment run by a Harvard professor will help.

In their research, Drs Todd Rogers and Jessica Lasky-Fink[7] sent 7,002 people emails about the same topic, but they sent half of the people a shorter version of the message. The goal was to see what the response and open rates were when only the length of the message changed.

Half the recipients received a 127-word message, and the other half got a fourty-nine word message. The only difference between the messages was that they cut out the information in the middle of the longer email. The beginning and the end were the same.

Neither of the emails was very long, but the results are surprising. What they found when they sent similar messages was that the long messages were opened less than half as often as the shorter messages. Not only were the read rates higher but more than twice as many people responded to the shorter email. Twice as many—that's significant. Imagine you could improve the read rate of your work emails by even a fraction of that amount!

- Original email - 127 words - 2.7% response rate
- Shorter email - 49 words - 4.8% response rate

The response rate for the shorter email was more than 60% higher than for the longer message. Using fewer words produced a better result.

You can see the text from the original email on the next page. The grey, crossed out text shows what Dr Todd Rogers and Jessica Lasky-Fink removed to create the shorter message.

Hello,

I'm a professor at Harvard studying opinions, decision-making goals, and expectations of school board members. ~~As a school board member, you have an important and difficult job. You and your fellow school board members are making critical decisions right now that will profoundly impact the lives of students, teachers, and families in your schools and communities. I know you are busy with many urgent and important decisions as your schools reopen. School district leaders like you are balancing many competing interests. Your participation will be very helpful in the research I am conducting.~~ I would like to learn from you how school district leaders are thinking about the challenges facing schools right now. Would you please complete this brief survey? The link is here https://surveylink.com

Thank you for your time,

Dr Todd Rogers
Professor of Public Policy

Why Do We Have Trouble Writing Short Emails?

Despite the research and our own experience showing us that people prefer shorter emails, we still write long emails. Why is that?

First, it takes effort to write a short message. A well-known quote that's attributed to multiple people from Mark Twain to Blaise Pascal[8], is "I would have written a shorter letter, but I did not have the time." It takes time and effort to organize and condense our thoughts into a summary. It is much easier to write what we're thinking, in whatever order it comes out, and then hit Send.

In addition to our natural desire to make things easier for ourselves, we write long emails because we assume that people need a lot of information. We think everyone needs the details on our topic to be better equipped to reply. We give people as much information as possible so they've got everything we think they need. We also add information to justify our actions, or to demonstrate how much thought, effort, or work we've put into a topic.

The problem is, not only is this based on the false assumption that people need lots of information to be able to do what we want but it also assumes first, they want the information and second, they don't already have it. Any time we spend writing information that people don't want, don't need, or already have reduces the chances our message will be read. It also wastes time for us and the reader.

If the goal is to write short emails, how do you know when you've written too much? How long is too long?

Unfortunately, there's no hard and fast rule for defining a "too long" email. It's going to depend on your situation and your topic. For context, long doesn't mean twenty pages. Long can be anything that requires scrolling to see all the content. Given that at least 40 percent[9] of work email—some say 60 percent[10]—is read on a mobile device, the need to scroll makes even short messages seem long. But as a rough rule of thumb, if the reader needs to use the scroll wheel on their mouse, or if the reader is scrolling through the message on their phone and have to swipe more than twice, the email is probably too long. If your message goes beyond that, try to make it shorter.

Of course, there are exceptions to this. If you're providing detailed instructions or writing about multiple topics, you probably need a longer email. But the goal should always be to make the message as short as possible. After all, it doesn't matter how valuable the message is if no one reads it.

What to Include in a Short Email

What most of us need in an email is just enough information to understand the message and take whatever action the sender wants us to take. For someone to be able to do what you want or need, they need to know a small number of things. We're going to add to these details that were covered in section one:

- The topic;
- The purpose of the email;
- What specific action or response you want from them;
- The time frame in which to do it;
- Just enough detail for them to understand the situation and move ahead with whatever they need to do; and
- Nothing that gets in the way or confuses the topic or purpose.

What people don't usually need is what you want to carefully avoid, including:

- Step-by-step descriptions of activities or events. Summarize the information or leave it out altogether.
- Thoughts and opinions about why such-and-such event occurred. State what happened and move on.
- Comprehensive explanations for why we are asking for something. A simple summary saying why you need something is sufficient.

There are many more things we don't need when receiving emails, but they all have a common theme. Don't include any information that isn't directly related to and necessary for the recipient to take the next step. If you have to include details, summarize them into key points.

Even when writing about a topic the reader is unfamiliar with, you can still cut out much of the detail. Most people will understand a summary and can get on with their work without lots of detail. And, in the event they need or want more information, they can always ask you for it.

How Short is Too Short?

Given all this talk about short emails being better emails, is there such a thing as too short? Well, in short, yes, there is. (Yes, that is a terrible pun. Sometimes I just can't help myself.)

The most common types of inappropriately short emails come from forwarded email chains. Any email that only says, "Here you go," or "FYI," is definitely too short. Beyond these frustrating examples, an email is too short if it doesn't contain the basic information the reader needs. If you haven't given the reader the topic, what they need to do, when to do it, and if they don't have the minimum necessary information to make a start, then the email is too short.

Use the list of what to include in a short email and use the fewest words possible to achieve what is needed and you'll have the minimum necessary when sending the first message in a conversation.

If you're worried about cutting out too much, include a statement like, "If you'd like more information about [XYZ], please let me know." This shows the reader you have more information and are happy to share it.

ACTIVITY
CAN YOU MAKE YOUR EMAILS SHORTER?

Find a long email you've sent recently. It needs to be the first email in a conversation and not a reply. If you haven't sent anything long, you can use a long email you've received from someone else. Look to see if any of the following things are in the email:

- Background information.
- Explanations saying why you are asking a question.
- Justifications for actions already taken.
- Step-by-step descriptions instead of summaries.
- Information not directly linked to the email purpose.

If you have included any of these items, consider what would happen if you took them out:

- Would the core message be the same?
- Would the email be clearer?
- Would the reader still know what they needed to do?

If your answers to the second set of questions are all YES, then you have found something you can remove and still have a clear email.

This evaluation not only helps review old emails to find what could be improved but also works for evaluating emails you will write in the future. If the email you are writing is long, repeat the activity above before hitting Send to see if there is anything you can remove.

You can download a copy of this activity here:
https://chrisfenning.com/resources/

WHITE SPACE MAKES EMAILS EASIER TO READ

Despite repeatedly saying short emails are better, there are times when you need to write a longer email.

The problem with long emails, even the ones that need to be long, isn't that they are long but that they are often badly structured. They are written in a way that is hard to read. Information is packed into long paragraphs. Questions are mixed with information and hard to find. And key information looks the same as all the rest of the text.

The structure and formatting of a long message can make a significant difference in how easy it is to read, and the longer the message, the more structure it needs.

The first step to improving a long email is to start with a good introduction as described in section one, to serve as a summary and introduction to the rest of the message. After that, the next most significant change is to use white space.

When we read, we are used to words that are crammed onto a page. Any fiction book or newspaper has small, densely packed words on every page. This is actually helpful when you're reading a story because the dense text requires you to focus more, and in turn, this focus keeps you immersed in the story page after page. Plus, from a purely financial perspective, more pages would mean more printing and thus a higher cost, so it is cheaper to have the highest number of words in the smallest number of pages.

While densely packed text works great in a novel, it's not great for work emails. Dense text is difficult to read *quickly*. And I think we can all agree that we don't have the luxury of time to slowly read every email we get at work. We must read and interpret emails quickly so we can get on with doing whatever it is the email asks us to do.

The easiest way to make messages quicker to read and interpret is to add white space, which means having some space between blocks of text on the page. Line breaks, new paragraphs, and blank lines are all examples of white space. It's easier to read three separate four-line paragraphs than one paragraph with twelve lines because it takes mental energy to keep track of the specific line we are reading in a long paragraph. Studies have shown that adding gaps between blocks of text on a page makes them faster to read because we don't need to concentrate as hard on keeping track of what we've read on the page.[11]

White space also helps us see the breaks in information, making it easier to scan an email and see changes in topics or see key information.

CASE STUDY: IMPROVING SAM'S EMAIL TO DIANE

Let's take a look at the main example we've used throughout the book so far—the email to Diane about website upgrades. The original message is a single block of text. By comparison, the second version includes more white space.

To	Diane@greatplacetowork.com
Subject	FW: FW: FW: RE: Ticket 87D55X

Hi Diane,
We've had calls and some emails from the product and customer service teams. They have a problem with some customers calling and messaging. Apparently there is a problem with the website and the login screen isn't working. I'm not sure exactly what it is because our team hasn't had time to look into the issue yet but I expect it will take us most of the week to analyze and fix it. We are fully booked for the rest of the month with all the new functionality you requested for the website. Anyway, the product team want us to look into the customer website issue, and they want us to do it today. I've included their messages in the email chain below. The full details of the login issue are in customer ticket #87D55X if you want to see the full detail. We are supposed to be supporting them, but, as I said, we are fully booked already. This is a problem for us, we can't do both things. That's why I'm writing to you, to ask for your help. I want to stop some of the work we had planned to give us time to look at the website issue. I think we can stop one of the three things

we are working on, that should give us enough time. The problem is I don't know what work to stop. You are the owner of the website upgrade and so I thought you could help me choose what to stop. Do you have a preference for what we keep working on and what we stop working on? We could stop any of these things: The layout changes for the sidebar menus on the home page. The automation for the pdf generation of customer bills. Or the ask a question form you wanted to add to the contact page. Which one can we stop working on? Does it matter? Or can I just make the choice myself. Apparently this is urgent and the product team wants us to look at it right away. If you can give me your answer in the next hour that would be great. Thank you.

| To | Diane@greatplacetowork.com |
| Subject | FW: FW: FW: RE: Ticket 87D55X |

We've had calls and some emails from the product and customer service teams. They have a problem with some customers calling and messaging. Apparently there is a problem with the website and the login screen isn't working.

I'm not sure exactly what the issue is because our team hasn't had time to look into the issue yet. We are fully booked for the rest of the month with all the new functionality you requested for the website.

Anyway, the product team wants us to look into the customer website issue, and they want us to do it today. I've included their messages in the email chain below. They have opened a ticket for tracing, it is #87D55X if you want to see the full detail. We are supposed to be supporting them, but, as I said, we are fully booked already. This is a problem for us, we can't do both things. That's why I'm writing to you, to ask for your help.

I want to stop some of the work we had planned to give us time to look at the website issue. I think we can stop one of the three things we are working on, that should give us enough time. The problem is I don't know what work to stop. You are the owner of the website upgrade and so I thought you could help me choose what to stop.

Do you have a preference for what we keep working on and what we stop working on? We could stop any of these things: The layout changes for the sidebar menus on the home page. The automation for the pdf generation of customer bills. Or the ask a question form you wanted to add to the contact page. Which one can we stop working on? Does it matter? Or can I just make the choice myself.

Apparently this is urgent and the product team wants us to look at it right away. If you can give me your answer in the next hour that would be great. Thank you.

Regards,
Sam

Looking at these two versions, which one is easier to read? The text in both is exactly the same. The only thing that's different is the addition of white space. By separating the text into short paragraphs and adding blank lines between them, the message becomes easier to read.

Bullet points & numbered lists

Another good way to break up dense blocks of text is with bullet points and/or numbered lists. These options help separate and organize information into easy-to-read lists.

We expect blocks of text to be written as sentences and have learned to absorb and interpret paragraphs by subconsciously looking for sentence structure. When we don't find familiar sentence structures in a paragraph, we have to work harder to interpret the information.

You may recognize this if you've ever tried to learn a foreign language. Even when you know the vocabulary, the different rules of grammar make it harder to read sentences because the words aren't in the order you expect. It's the same when you find a list in the middle of a paragraph. Without a recognizable sentence structure, it is harder to read. It's far easier to absorb and interpret a list of items when it's split into a list.

Take a look at this example. This block of text contains a list of things that need to be done. Can you see where they are?

To	Rob@greatplacetowork.com
Subject	Planning & next steps for the off-site event in March

Hi Rob,

Sarah approved the off-site event next month. We need to start planning to make sure everything is ready in time. Here are some things I thought we should start; Check the team schedule doesn't have any conflicts with major client meetings. Confirm the location is available on the dates we want. Find out if anyone on the team has special dietary needs. Check if we need to rent cars to get there or if the company minibus and driver are available. Finalize the budget. I'm sure there's more we need to look into but this is a good place to start. Let me know what you'd like to start with and if we should anything to this list.

Thank you!

Sam

Without bullet points, you need to read the whole paragraph and mentally organize the information into a list as you go. While it might not be the hardest thing in the world, it still takes effort and concentration. If you quickly scanned this message, you might not even notice there is a list at all.

Adding bullet points makes the list much clearer. Looking at the updated version, it's immediately obvious that the message contains a list. This makes it easier to read and quicker to scan. Plus, Rob is more likely to identify tasks to add because he can clearly see all the other tasks in the list.

To	Rob@greatplacetowork.com
Subject	Planning & next steps for the off-site event in March

Hi Rob,

Sarah approved the off-site event next month. We need to start planning to make sure everything is ready in time. Here are some things I thought we should start:

- Check the team schedule doesn't have any conflicts with major client meetings.
- Confirm the location is available on the dates we want.
- Find out if anyone on the team has special dietary needs.
- Check if we need to rent cars to get there or if the company minibus and driver are available.
- Finalize the budget.

I'm sure there's more we need to look into but this is a good place to start. Let me know what you'd like to start with and if we should anything to this list.

Thank you!
Sam

Numbered lists, also known as ordered lists, have an additional benefit. Not only do they separate items into an easy-to-read list but they make it easier for someone to reply.

If Sam had numbered the tasks instead of using bullets, Rob could have replied with this.

Hi Sam,

I think we should start with #2 because if the location isn't available it impacts everything else we need to plan. After that, we can do the rest in the following order: 1, 5, 3, 4.

I'll have a think about what else we need to do and will send you my notes before 3pm today.

Thanks,
Rob

[from original message…]
1. Check the team schedule doesn't have any conflicts with major client meetings.
2. Confirm the location is available on the dates we want.
3. Find out if anyone on the team has special dietary needs.
4. Check if we need to rent cars to get there or if the company minibus and driver are available.
5. Finalize the budget.

Instead of having to write long sentences to clarify which item to do first, Rob could reference the number of the item in Sam's original email.

Numbered lists are also a great way to be clear about the priority of the items in your lists when that matters.

To see more good examples of this method check out Attention Management expert Maura Thomas's short video and blog here: _https://maurathomas.com/business-email-writing-tips/_

RULES FOR QUESTIONS, ACTIONS & DECISIONS

When it comes to layout and formatting, the questions, actions, and decisions in your emails require special attention.

Why is this? The more important the information, the greater the visibility it needs to ensure it draws the appropriate attention, and questions, actions, and decisions are usually pretty high in order of importance.

Make Questions, Actions & Decisions Stand Out

To make your questions, actions, and decisions stand out, apply these three tips:

1. Put them on their own lines.
2. Label them.
3. Use formatting.

Don't bury a question in the middle of a paragraph. Pull it out and give it its own line. The same with actions and decisions.

Having a single line does call our attention to a question, particularly if there's a white space before and after it, but if that single line also starts with the word "Question," "Action" or "Decision," it'll be easier to identify those as key pieces of information when scanning the email.

Using formatting to call extra attention to the question, action, or decision helps these items stand out from paragraphs, indicating they are different from just information.

To give you a really clear idea of just how impactful these three tips can be, let's start with a block of text that includes a question.

> The client is pleased with the progress we've made.
> They want to extend the contract for another six months. This is not something I usually approve by myself but the client wanted an answer then and there. So I decided we would extend the contract. I know this means a lot of extra work for the team but I couldn't turn down such a valuable contract. Can you schedule a meeting with the whole team next week? I want to talk to them about the additional workload and start finding ways to deliver before we get too busy.

Can you see the question? How long did it take you to find it?

Unless you are especially good at spotting question marks at a glance, you probably had to search the text to find the question. Including questions inside paragraphs hides them.

To avoid this issue, bring the questions out onto their own line. Here is the same block of text but with the question on a separate line and some white space above and below.

> The client is pleased with the progress we've made. They want to extend the contract for another six months. This is not something I usually approve by myself but the client wanted an answer then and there. So I decided we would extend the contract. I know this means a lot of extra work for the team but I couldn't turn down such a valuable contract.
>
> Can you schedule a meeting with the whole team next week?
>
> I want to talk to them about the additional workload and start finding ways to deliver before we get too busy.

How long did it take you to find the question this time? I bet it was much faster and also much easier.

The second tip tells us to add labels. Putting the label "question" before a question makes it clear the line is a question. Yes, the presence of a question mark at the end of the sentence does the same thing, but we won't see that until the end of the sentence.

Also, when scanning an email, we read the first few words of each paragraph and skim the rest. (Yes, I say scanning a lot, but that's because we do it a lot…) Putting a label at the start of a question, action, or decision increases the likelihood that the reader will see it and read it. A question someone sees is much more likely to be answered than a question they don't see.

The client is pleased with the progress we've made. They want to extend the contract for another six months. This is not something I usually approve by myself but the client wanted an answer then and there. So I decided we would extend the contract. I know this means a lot of extra work for the team but I couldn't turn down such a valuable contract.

Question: Can you schedule a meeting with the whole team next week?

I want to talk to them about the additional workload and start finding ways to deliver before we get too busy.

The third tip adds formatting to the text. In the example above, applying the bold format to the label makes it stand out even more. It draws your eye straight to it and you know where to look on the page. And as the sender of this email, there's one thing I want you to do—answer the question. So, I'm going to make it stand out.

Some people like to go a step further to make questions stand out by adding bullet points, ordered lists, and headings as shown in the next two examples.

Question: Can you schedule a meeting with the whole team next week?
Question: Do you have any suggestions for how to break the news to the team?

Questions:

1. Can you schedule a meeting with the whole team next week?
2. Do you have any suggestions for how to break the news to the team?

I recommend this if you have multiple questions listed together, but if it is just a single question, a label should be enough.

While all the examples here show questions, the same approach works for actions and decisions.

NOTE: Some email systems turn all emails into plain text, meaning all the formatting is striped out. When this happens, the use of bold formatting to highlight important information won't work. This makes it even more important to use white space and labels to make them stand out. If your corporate email system converts everything to plain text, try using upper-case letters for the labels instead of bold formatting. That will help make the words stand out. For example, question becomes QUESTION, and action becomes ACTION.

How to Structure Questions, Actions & Decisions

You've just seen how adding labels and formatting will make questions, actions, and decisions stand out so readers will see there is something important in the email. Next, there are a few extra steps you should take to make the content of these messages crystal clear.

The way you write these three important sentences can increase (or decrease) the chance of recipients understanding them. It can also increase the chance of getting an answer or having people take the action.

The Format for a Question

Most of us know how to write a question, so I won't explain that, but when writing an email to more than one person, there is one thing you can do to increase the chance of getting an answer from the right person. Start each question by addressing the person who should give the answer. If you don't add a name, everyone who gets the email might assume someone else will answer, or you could get an answer from someone who isn't the right or best person to do so.

Write questions in the following format: [Name of person] + [question] as shown in the next example.

Questions:

- **Rajesh**, can you send me the team's status updates on the Pinky project?
- **Emma, Sajhid, Neil,** can you please update the comments in your sections of the contract by the end of the week?
- **Neil,** can you send me a progress report on Friday?

Note how the names are formatted in bold font, making it even easier to see who the question is for. Be careful not to over-format the email, but bolding a few names shouldn't cause a problem.

The Format for an Action

When writing an action, you need to say who will do what and by when. This simple structure ensures there is no confusion.

Write actions in the following format: [Name of person] will [statement about the specific task or activity] by [deadline] as shown in the next example.

Actions:
- **Dave** will share the report before the next client meeting which is at 10am Friday 18th September.
- **Santosh** will fix the last three bugs by Tuesday afternoon at 3pm.
- **Rebecca** will contact Clive to confirm the priority order of the projects before our next meeting.

When writing an action, the more specific the information, the better. Anyone reading a who-what-when statement will quickly see if the action is for them, what action must happen, and the time frame for it to happen.

The Format for a Decision

Since decision-makers have the authority to make decisions (or at least you would hope they do), when a decision is communicated by email, the minimum you need to include is who made the decision and what was decided. There is rarely a need to include the justification or reasoning behind a decision, but if you do, make sure to follow the advice earlier in this section about writing shorter emails.

Write decisions in the following format: [Who] + [What was decided] as shown in the next example.

Decisions:
- **Amy** decided that the project will end tomorrow.
- **Dan** decided to fund the project for another three months.
- **Bhargavi** decided to add three more developers to complete the task on time.

You don't need to use this exact format. You could write the decision followed by the name of the person making it, for example. What's important is that it's clear to the reader what the decision is and who made it.

NOTE: When sending messages to groups, it helps to write the first and last names of people named in each question, action, or decision. This avoids the situation of asking Dan to do something and the recipients having to ask, "Which Dan?"

Answering Other People's Questions

Now that you've learned how to make questions stand out in your emails, you should know it is equally important to make answers stand out when replying to other people.

Here are two ways you can make your answers stand out when replying to questions in emails:

1. Repeat their questions in your reply; and
2. Answer in line using a different color font.

Repeat the Questions in Your Reply

When answering someone else's question, copy the question, paste it in your reply, and then write the answer. It doesn't matter how they wrote the questions in their message. They could be buried in a paragraph or made clear each on its own line with a label. However they've done it, copy the question and put it in your reply, and then answer the question. Don't just give an answer by itself. Doing this makes it clear what question has been asked and if there are multiple questions, which reply relates to each question.

This has two benefits:

1. It's clear to you what question you are answering; and
2. It is obvious which part of your email is an answer to their question.

Imagine you received an email with three questions. If you reply with three answers without repeating the question, the recipient needs to spend time working out which answers go with each question. They also need to separate the answers from any other information you may have shared, such as the introduction, extra detail, or your own questions for them. By repeating their original question and then answering it, it's faster for the reader to find what they need. It's going to be crystal clear which answer relates to each of the questions that were asked.

Here is an example:

To	Nidhi@greatplacetowork.com
Subject	[CONFIDENTIAL] Project Clipper news and 2 questions

Hi Nidhi,

I've just heard the project is being stopped at the end of the week. I know this is a big deal but I don't have all the details yet so please keep this to yourself for now.

The next thing we have to do is work out how we tell the team. Can you help me with a couple of things?

1. **Question**: Can you schedule a meeting with the whole team tomorrow?
2. **Question**: Do you have any suggestions for how to break the news to the team?

We can talk more about this when I see you this afternoon. In the meantime, I'll be working out how we can keep the team together.

Sorry to be the bearer of bad news.
Aaron

Nidhi can reply like this:

To	Aaron@greatplacetowork.com
Subject	Re. [CONFIDENTIAL] Project Clipper news and 2 questions

Hi Aaron,

That's really bad news. I have so many questions but I'll keep them until we talk later.

To answer your questions:

1. **Question**: Can you schedule a meeting with the whole team tomorrow?
   - YES – I'll set something up first thing in the morning. You'll get an invitation in the next hour.

2. **Question**: Do you have any suggestions for how to break the news to the team?
   - I have some ideas but want to think about it before sharing them. We can talk more about them this afternoon.

If there's anything else I can do, let me know.

Speak later,
Nidhi

For the sake of space in the book, I've kept this example short. This may make the approach seem a little redundant, but keep in mind that the longer the original email, the more valuable it is to repeat the entire question in your reply.

Answer Inline Using Different Color Font

An alternative to duplicating the question is to write your answer in the location of the question in the original email and then change the color of the text to make it stand out. This approach is often characterized by a statement like, "See my answer in blue following your question(s)." The original sender then scrolls down the message to see your replies.

I used to do this, and it saved me time because I didn't have to find and copy all the questions. I could just read the original email and reply whenever I saw a question. However, there is a problem with this approach—color doesn't show up if the recipient uses plain text emails.

This may sound like an unusual scenario, but it does happen. I stopped using this approach when colleagues in partner companies told me their company email system converted everything to plain text. While I'd thought the color made it easier to see, they couldn't easily distinguish my reply from the rest of the text.

If you want to avoid this problem, use the first method of repeating the question in your reply.

Separating information using headings

If your email contains a lot of information, use headings to break it up. Earlier you saw how paragraphs make it easier to read dense text by breaking it into smaller pieces. There is a limit to how helpful paragraphs can be, though. Too many paragraphs, even short ones, are still difficult to read. Remember, we scan long emails rather than read every word.

To help your reader, add headings or subtitles to the message that divides the content into small sections and shows the reader what each section contains.

For example, adding simple headings like **Problem description**, **Proposed solution**, and **Next steps** to an email will show the reader what each section contains.

An example of how to use headings is shown in the next few pages.

Too much formatting is bad

Don't go crazy with the formatting. Too much formatting can actually make a message harder to read. A variety of different styles is confusing and distracting. The reader won't know which format style indicates importance, a change in topic, and so on.

Too much formatting also causes problems for anyone using software to convert visual material into audio format. Text-to-speech software has to describe all the formatting, and not only does it take time but too much formatting will make it harder to understand the message.

So use formatting sparingly. The specific advice in this section about separating topics, labeling questions, actions, and decisions, provides the right amount of formatting for most emails.

CASE STUDY: IMPROVING SAM'S EMAIL TO DIANE

Let's take a look at the impact layout and formatting can have on a long email. Earlier in this section, you saw how the addition of white space improved the readability of Sam's message to Diane. Now you'll see how to improve it farther by adding a few headings, an ordered list, and a label for the question.

To	Diane@greatplacetowork.com
Subject	[URGENT] Website upgrades – Need help choosing one to stop

Hi Diane,

We've had calls and some emails from the product and customer service teams. They have a problem with some customers calling and messaging. Apparently there is a problem with the website and the login screen isn't working. I'm not sure exactly what the issue is because our team hasn't had time to look into the issue yet.

Our team can't support all the work requests
We are fully booked for the rest of the month with all the new functionality you requested for the website.

Anyway, the product team wants us to look into the customer website issue, and they want us to do it today. I've included their messages in the email chain below. They have opened a ticket for tracing, it is #87D55X if you want to see the full detail. We are supposed to be supporting them, but, as I said, we are fully booked already. This is a problem for us, we can't do both things. That's why I'm writing to you, to ask for your help.

Proposed solution – Stop working on one of the planned upgrades
I want to stop some of the work we had planned to give us time to look at the website issue. I think we can stop one of the three things we are working on, that should give us enough time. The problem

is I don't know what work to stop. You are the owner of the website upgrade and so I thought you could help me choose what to stop.

Do you have a preference for what we keep working on and what we stop working on? We could stop any of these things:

1. The layout changes for the sidebar menus on the home page.
2. The automation for the pdf generation of customer bills.
3. The ask a question form you wanted to add to the contact page.

Question: Which one can we stop working on? Does it matter? Or can I just make the choice myself.

Next steps:
Apparently this is urgent and the product team wants us to look at it right away. If you can give me your answer in the next hour that would be great. Thank you.

Regards,
Sam

Which one is easier to read, the original email or this one with a little extra formatting?

FORMATTING MULTI-TOPIC EMAILS

One common reason for long emails is the need to include multiple topics, which in turn will need more structure. I'll say that again, multiple topics need more structure. This is because when you've got different topics, you don't want them to blend together. You want the reader to be able to identify where one topic ends and the next topic begins.

There are some simple ways to do this:

1. Write a good introduction.
2. Use whitespace, sub-headings, and formatting.

If you've introduced your email well by saying there are two topics, it is simpler to keep them apart in the message. But the introduction isn't enough. You need to make it easy for the reader to see the break between topics. Otherwise, they might miss the transition and the information won't make sense to them.

Yes, this is the reader's problem, they should read slower and pay better attention. But it is also your problem if they don't understand your message or don't reply to all of your questions. So instead of expecting the reader to do better, you can make it easier for them by using white space, sub-headings, and formatting to separate the topics.

Here's an example showing a simple way to separate topics.

To	Nidhi@Projectoffice.com
Subject	Project Everest – Questions about project lead and budget

Hi Nidhi,

Can you help me with a couple of things on Project Everest? The first is a decision about who should lead the project. The second is a question about the project budget deadlines. The questions and more info for each topic are given below. If you can get back to me before the end of Thursday I'd really appreciate it. Thanks.

Topic 1: Who should lead the project?
Blah blah blah blah blah blah blah blah blah blah blah blah blah blah blah blah blah blah Blah blah blah blah blah blah blah blah blah blah blah blah blah blah blah Blah blah blah blah blah blah blah blah blah blah blah

Action: blah blah blah blah blah Blah blah blah blah blah blah blah blah blah blah blah blah blah blah blah

Topic 2: Budget deadline questions
Blah blah blah blah blah blah blah blah blah blah blah blah blah blah blah blah blah blah Blah blah blah blah blah blah blah blah blah blah

Question: blah blah blah blah blah Blah blah blah
Question: blah blah blah blah blah blah blah blah blah blah blah blah

Blah blah blah blah blah blah blah blah blah blah blah blah blah blah blah Blah blah blah blah blah blah blah blah blah blah blah blah blah blah Blah blah blah blah blah blah blah blah blah blah blah blah blah blah blah

Thanks,
Paulo

Even at a glance, you can clearly see the message contains two different topics. For the sake of space in this book, I've not included all the detail for each topic, but you can imagine each one was well-written with labeled questions and a clear purpose.

The example has white space, line breaks, and sub-headings that are formatted in bold, all of which are good practices for a longer email.

There's also something more—each topic has a clear label that says "Topic 1" and "Topic 2". With the sub-headings labeled like this, it's almost impossible to miss the fact that there are two topics in the message and the transition between them is equally obvious.

Also notice the introduction. Paulo makes it clear that the theme is Project Everest and there are two topics he wants help with. If you've introduced email by saying how many topics you are writing about, the reader is going to be primed to look for two topics. Then, when they review the email, the formatting makes it clear where Topic 1 begins and ends, and the same for Topic 2.

NOTE: I refer to "both" or "two" topics in this section, but this approach works no matter how many topics are in the email. It could be two, three, seven, or more. Hopefully not more though, because that's too much to have in one email. If you have seven topics, split them into separate emails.

USING GRAPHICS & IMAGES IN EMAILS

As the saying goes, a picture is worth a thousand words. Therefore, if our goal is to have shorter emails, it makes sense to exchange 1,000 words for a single image. Right? Well, while this sounds good in theory, it's not quite that simple.

There are some benefits to adding images to an email, like:

- A picture is worth a thousand words.
- Pictures provide rich information in a small space.
- Easier to interpret (usually).
- Creates impact.
- Improves reading and engagement.

Looking at this list, it would seem obvious that, when possible, we should use images to make our messages clearer for recipients. Unfortunately, adding images in emails can cause a few problems, like:

- Images don't always download or open.
- Corporate email systems can remove images.
- Images might not format well on mobile devices.

First, the images don't always download and open automatically. If you've ever seen the "Right click to download images" notification, you'll know what I'm talking about. The email looks messy and there are warning symbols that immediately make people suspicious of the content. While it only takes a couple of clicks to download the images, that is an extra step the reader might not take. If they don't, they are left with the words in your email, which may or may not make sense without the image.

Figure 5: Images don't always display in emails

The second issue is that some company email servers strip out images from emails. This may be to reduce storage space on their servers, to reduce the risk of viruses, or simply because that's how the email system has always been configured. Whatever the reason, there is a chance your image won't make it to recipients.

The last issue is that the image may be difficult to see on a small screen. Not every email client supports zooming in or expanding an image. If this happens, your attempt to be clear becomes frustrating for a reader who is squinting at a tiny image on their phone or trying to figure out how to view a huge image on a smaller screen. So while it is helpful to use images, you need to balance that against the risk that your message won't get through.

My advice about using images in emails is this:

1. See what the people around you do. If all your colleagues and clients are embedding images in their emails, then consider if you should too.
2. Add the image as an attachment instead of embedding it in the email. This means your email message must be clear by itself and the attachments provides additional information.
3. Only add images if it adds value and strengthens the message. Never add them just for the sake of it.

USE ATTACHMENTS & LINKS

Attachments and links are a great way to provide detail while also keeping an email short and easy to read.

By now you know that structure, layout, and formatting help make long emails easier to read, but instead of letting the formatting do all the heavy lifting, it's better to write a shorter email in the first place.

If the recipient needs lots of information to understand the topic and achieve the email's purpose, don't put the detail in the body of the email. As you saw earlier, long emails are read less often and are scanned quickly. Instead of putting everything in the body of the email, direct the reader to additional sources of information, such as attachments and links to documents stored elsewhere. This increases the chance that they will read your message while still giving them access to everything they need. That's a win-win.

Supporting data, documents, and background information are all good things to put in an attachment. People can read them if they want or need to but aren't forced to wade through it all in the email.

How to Effectively Use Attachments

Whenever you include an attachment, here are some simple rules to follow:

- **DO** tell the recipient why there is an attachment.
- **DO** say what's in the attachment.
- **DO** say why they need to read it.
- **DO** name attachments clearly.
- **DO** check if the attachment is small enough to send.
- **DON'T** leave key information in the attachment (**DO** add it to the email).

If your message doesn't explicitly reference the attachment, there's a good chance the reader won't open it. Research shows only 6 percent of email attachments are opened.[12] That means nineteen out of twenty people won't ever read the documents you send. This doesn't mean you should put everything into the email instead of attachments. The main email still needs to be clear and concise. What it does mean is that when you include an attachment, you absolutely must make sure you explain why the reader needs to read it.

Thinking about it another way, if you don't explain what the attachment contains and its purpose, why would someone know they need to open it? Think about your own experience for a moment. Do you open every attachment sent to you via email? If you open any of them, what causes you to do so? Remember for every email you send, there is a receiver—like you—who needs to read and respond to it.

Just like writing a good subject line, your attachments must be explained with a clear topic and purpose. They also need to be easy to identify. Name the attachments clearly and use those file names in the email. It is quite frustrating to have four attachments where none of the file names obviously relate to the topic being discussed. How will your recipient know which attachment to open while addressing each topic in the email without that correlation?

Email systems have limitations on attachment sizes. If your attachment is over 5 MB, check to see if it can be sent. It may seem like a pain to search for that information, but taking a few minutes to check the system limitations can save you much more time in the long run. The alternative is to blindly hope it gets through only to find out later that it never made it. If you can't find the size limitation information, send the attachment and then ask the recipient if it arrived. A quick phone call or instant message will tell you if it arrived or if you need to find an alternative method to share the large file.

The final rule is about not leaving key information in the attachment. If the attachment contains critical information, make sure you also put it, or a summary of it, into the body of the email. You can then direct the reader to the attachment to get more details.

Exception to the Rule

A possible exception to these rules comes into play if you know for certain that the recipient wants all the detail. You can put it in the body of the email, but you need to be *100% sure* they want all the detail. If it turns out they don't really like details, you'll reduce the chance of them reading what you send. If you are sure the other person wants all the info, you should write a summary first and then write the detail after. This gives the reader a good introduction and overview so they don't have to read everything to understand the overall message.

Using Hyperlinks Instead of URLs

An alternative to attachments is to include links to other sources of information. Hyperlinks are a great way to send information. You don't need to worry about email size limits because the file isn't included with the message, and this also avoids the pain of opening the attachment on a mobile device. Plus, there are fewer issues with version control, especially if you link to a document that is regularly updated.

Hyperlinks also save money for your company because they reduce the amount of data that is sent by email.[13] If you send a 5 MB attachment to five people, that is 25 MB of storage somewhere on an email server. If the document is forwarded multiple times or sent back and forth, those data volumes really start to add up.

When using links, there are three things to consider:

1. Make sure it's a hyperlink and not a text URL.
2. Know where to put the link.
3. Consider if everyone has access to the file.

URLs are often long and complicated. If you share a link in an email, don't just paste a long URL but instead make it a clickable hyperlink. If you don't do this, it's harder for the person receiving the message to access that URL. They will have to highlight it, copy it, and paste it into a browser, and if they don't do that correctly, it might not take them to the right place. Plus, everyone expects links to be clickable. Make things easier for your reader by using clickable hyperlinks.

If the link is a long string of random letters and numbers, consider writing "click this link" and making the words clickable by embedding the URL in that text string. This looks neater, saves space in the email, and reduces the risk of incorrectly copying the long URL.

If you are wondering where to put the links, put them in the relevant place in the message. There is no need to list them all together in the introduction or gather them all at the end. Put them where the reader needs to see them in your message.

And finally, make sure the link directs the user to an accessible location. If you've gotten as far as getting someone to click on the link, how annoyed will they be if they can't access the file? Common causes are files in restricted folders, or on a team-specific SharePoint site, and when an internal file link is shared with someone outside the company. Be sure the link is accessible and test the link before you send it.

Use Templates for Recurring Emails

Recurring emails are an opportunity for email efficiency. When I say recurring emails, I don't mean you're sending the exact same content. I'm talking about sending the same style of email with a similar purpose on a recurring basis. Examples of this include weekly report emails, team updates, and so on.

The first benefit of templates is that they save time. If you use a template, you don't need to start from scratch every time. The layout and formatting are already created. You can just drop the new information into the template and hit Send.

The second benefit of templates is that they make it easier for the recipient to read and absorb the information. Think about it, if the weekly update from your team leader always follows the same format, you'll become familiar with that format and know where to look for the important information. New projects are going to be included in one area; policy updates will be in another; decisions, actions, and questions will always look the same; and so forth. If your manager specifically asks you a question in the team update email, you will more easily and quickly recognize it if they use the same format every week, built into their template.

The third benefit of using a template is that you can also improve the template over time. The first time you send a recurring message, you might get some feedback about the content. Or the team may all ask questions about a particular section, which shows you it isn't clear enough. You can use that feedback to update the template so next time it's better. Then every time you send the template, you can improve it and give the audience what they need and want to receive. In the long run, this will save you all time.

The final benefit of using templates for recurring messages is when you go on vacation. If you send a weekly message, there's a good chance someone else will need to send that message while you are away. If you use a template, it makes the work simpler for whoever writes and sends it on your behalf and you can count on it being more true to what your people are used to receiving from you. Everyone will thank you for it!

How to Use Templates

You have a few options when it comes to creating templates for recurring emails:

1. Save a draft copy of the email and then copy that and use it whenever you send your weekly email message.
2. Copy the last email you sent and update it to fill in the blanks.
3. Create a template in a document (MS Word or equivalent) and then copy and paste it into the email and update it with new information.

There are pros and cons for each of these, and you may have your own preference for how to do this, but they are all easy ways to create a template.

When you have a good template, you not only save time creating the emails but it is also easier for your audience to receive and understand that information.

ASSESSMENT
HOW DO YOU STRUCTURE YOUR EMAILS?

For this self-assessment activity, find the last three to five long emails you sent. These can be the start of a conversation or part of an email chain. The important part is the length of the emails, so choosing ones that required the recipient to scroll to read all of them will work best for this activity.

Are the paragraphs short (less than four lines or six sentences)?	Yes/No/ Sometimes
Do you use bullets or numbered lists whenever possible?	Yes/No/ Sometimes
Do you use headings or text formatting to separate topics?	Yes/No/ Sometimes
Are questions, actions, and decisions on their own lines?	Yes/No/ Sometimes
Are questions, actions, and decisions clearly labeled?	Yes/No/ Sometimes
(If the email is a recurring topic) Have you used the same format/template for each of the regular recurring emails?	Yes/No/ Sometimes
Considering the answers above, are your emails as short as possible?	Yes/No/ Sometimes
Are all the URLs clickable hyperlinks?	Yes/No/ Sometimes

THINGS TO CONSIDER

If you circled YES for each question, well done, you start your emails clearly. If any of your answers are NO or SOMETIMES, your emails might not be as effective as you want. Longer emails with dense text are harder to read and research shows people are less likely to read them at all.

For any of the questions you didn't answer YES to, consider what changes you can make to improve the brevity and clarity of your message.

What specific parts of your email structure do you need to improve?

_____

_____

_____

_____

_____

_____

_____

_____

You can download a copy of this assessment here: https://chrisfenning.com/resources/

SECTION 3:
GROUP EMAILS, EMAIL CHAINS & FORWARDING

KEY POINTS

Group emails must have a clear purpose for all recipients; otherwise, they will be ignored or filed for later. To make the purpose clear, do the following:

- Have a clear subject line and introduction.
- Say why the group is getting the message.
- State the purpose of the message for each subgroup. *(If there are sub-groups)*
- Define any rules you want for how people reply *(i.e., is it okay to "reply all")*.

Cc'ing People

People interpret the Cc field in different ways. They may not treat it the way you intend. To avoid problems, follow these steps:

- Don't use the Cc field. Put everyone in the To field and explain why they are included in the group.
- If you do Cc people, explain why in the introduction.
- Don't be passive-aggressive by copying other people's managers without explaining why.

Bcc'ing People

There are two legitimate reasons to use Bcc. Anything else can be interpreted as being sneaky.

1. Protecting the privacy and data of the recipients by hiding their details.
2. Copying yourself on a message.

FORWARDING EMAIL CHAINS

- Always add an introduction.
- Change the subject line to include the purpose for the new recipient.
- Summarize the content of the chain rather than make the new recipient dig for information.
- Never forward with just an "FYI."

ADDING & REMOVING PEOPLE FROM EMAIL CHAINS

- Explain to the group why you added or removed recipients.
- Inform the added recipients why they have been added to the email.
- Inform removed participants why they have been removed in a separate email.
- Check with the email chain owner before removing people they've included, unless there's a level or urgency, in which case make the change and then talk to the sender of the original email.
- If other people change the recipients, find out why before reacting. There may be a good reason.

KEEPING EMAIL CHAINS ON TOPIC

- If an email chain has drifted off-topic or introduced a new topic, reset the conversation with a summary.
- Move new topics to new email chains and start a new subject line with topic and purpose.

MOVING COMMUNICATION BEYOND EMAIL

If an email conversation changes to a new channel (meeting, call, etc.) always close the loop with the rest of the group so that everyone is kept up to date.

INTRODUCTION

Group emails introduce a whole new world of problems for clear communication at work. Keeping the conversation on track, what to do when you are Cc'd, and how to add recipients can all be causes for confusion and/or frustration. In this section, you'll find advice and best practices to help keep your group emails organized, on track, and frustration-free.

It starts with how to introduce a group email and the nuances specific to group messages, which will build on what you learned in section one.

Then you'll discover why using the Carbon Copy (Cc) field causes problems in group messages, as well as the only two reasons you should ever use the Blind Copy (Bcc) field.

You'll also learn some simple but effective best practices for email chains, focusing on what to do when you add people, remove people, forward the chain, and so on.

Finally, you'll see what to do when the discussion moves beyond email. Often we will start a group conversation by email and then change the medium to instant messages, talking on the phone, or in person. You'll learn how to make sure those discussions end clearly for everyone involved.

And as with the previous sections, there are activities and assessments you can use to evaluate your progress and see how these techniques apply to you and your work.

INTRODUCING GROUP EMAILS

It's not unusual to send emails to more than one person, and adding even just one more person makes it a group email.

The first thing to do when writing a group email is to have a clear subject line and introduction. This means following all of the rules and methods you learned about in section one, so here's a reminder of those key points:

- The subject line must state the topic and purpose of the email.
- The first lines must deliver everything necessary to introduce and set up the message. These are:
  - What the message is about;
  - What the reader must do;
  - The key information; and
  - Relevant time frames.

In addition, the introduction to a group email must make it clear, explicitly stating, why the group is getting the message. While there is always a reason for including everyone, if you're hoping the recipients will automatically know what that reason is, you'll be disappointed. In most cases, replies only come from a small number of people in the group and some recipients won't read the message at all.

If the reason isn't clear, the recipients may think, *This is just a group update, I'll read it later.* How much later, and if they even read it, is anyone's guess.

Other common thoughts when receiving a group message include:

- Why did everyone need to get this?
- Why aren't you talking to people individually about the topic?
- I don't need to reply because someone else will answer the questions.
- Do I even need to read this?
- Perhaps I can ignore this because someone else in the group will reply…

If you don't want people to have these thoughts, you need to introduce the group email clearly.

This becomes even more important when you send a message to different groups of people in the same email. When you send a message to your team, it's obvious to the people receiving it that the team is the link between the recipients. But if the recipients don't often work together, or don't know each other at all, the link between recipients is much less clear. And when things are unclear, we tend to move to the next email in our inbox that is easier to understand.

Here's an example of how to introduce a group email. This message is going to a group of five different people.

To	'Project X mailing list'
Subject	New project starting – please read and start the next steps

Hi team,

Here is information about a new project we've been asked to support. You are all going to work on this and will need to be familiar with the information.

David & Irina, please review the information and create a list of questions you need answers to before the kick-off.

Gemma, Siyana, Vlad, can you start creating the usual kick-off documents?

Here's the info we've been sent so far … blah blah blah blah blah blah blah blah blah blah blah blah blah blah blah blah blah blah blah blah blah

First, there's an introduction that follows the rules we covered earlier in this book. Then the group is told why they are receiving the email. "You are all going to work on this and will need to be familiar with the information." No one should be wondering why they are getting this message.

Then there are two lines that talk to each of the different subgroups. The use of white space and text formatting shows us that one group is David and Irina and the second group is

Gemma, Siyana, and Vlad. Each group is clearly identified, and there's a specific request and reason why they have received the email.

Below that would be all the information about the project, but I've kept it out of the example since it's not relevant to make the point.

Introducing a group email this way addresses each of the separate subgroups and makes it clear to each group why they are receiving the message. Being clear right away about the reason they were included in a group email avoids recipients having to wonder unnecessarily about the purpose. Not only that, but if anyone in the group email was curious (or suspicious) about why other people are included, they don't need to waste time speculating if the reason is laid out in the introduction.

Establish How the Group Should Reply

Group emails don't always need group replies. When ten people reply to a group message, the volume and order of replies can clog up our already crowded inboxes.

To help reduce the number of emails sent in reply to a group message, here's a final tip:

- Say if it's okay to Reply All or not.

If you are sharing information and don't need a group discussion about it, you can tell the group not to Reply All by making a simple statement like this, "If you have any questions, please reply to me directly. Do not Reply All." Sure, some recipients may not read that and still send a group reply, but one line like this can significantly reduce the volume of replies to the group.

Alternatively, if you do want the group to all be aware of questions and comments about your original message, you could say that in your first email. Write something like, "If you have questions or feedback, please include the whole group in your reply so we can all benefit from the discussion."

Another way to handle group replies is to shift the conversation to another channel. If your team uses a group message system like Slack, you can ask for replies and questions to be posted there. Another option is to ask people to save their questions for the next scheduled meeting.

The key thing is, if you have an opinion about using or not using Reply All, then make that statement in your initial email.

THE PROBLEM WITH CC'ING

When you send a group email, you have the option to include people in the Cc line, which stands for Carbon Copy. Fun history fact: This term comes from the days when handwritten or printed forms could be duplicated by the use of carbon paper between two pages, which worked by pressing ink onto an extra sheet of paper on the bottom at the same time as writing or typing on the top page.[14]

In an email, the Cc field is usually the line just below the To field.

Figure 6: The Cc field is usually directly below the "to" field

The function of the Cc field is to add more recipients, so whether someone is in the To field or the Cc field, they both get the same email.

While the function of the Cc field is obvious, the purpose is less clear. What is it used for and when shouldn't we use it? These seem like simple questions to answer, but they are not.

Why not? Because there are no standard rules for Cc'ing. Different companies treat the Cc field differently. Different teams treat it differently. And even different people within the same team interpret, understand, and use the Cc field in different ways.

Here are some interpretations I've heard for what being "copied" on an email means:

- If I'm Cc'd, I don't need to read it. I file it away for later, just in case.
- Cc means I should read the message, but I'm not meant to reply.
- Cc tells me I'm on standby in case I'm needed for some future message in the conversation.

There are plenty of other interpretations too, and that is the problem. When there are no standard rules, whatever you believe the Cc line is for probably doesn't match the understanding of the people you send emails to. You can't be sure they're going to use it in the way you intend.

Here's an example to illustrate what I mean. You send an email to a few people in your team, telling them about a change in the priority of the tasks for next week. The main recipients will need to change their work order in line with the new priorities. You also Cc Adam because you want him to be aware of what's happening in the team, so he is prepared if anyone needs extra help. You don't need him to do anything and don't need a reply but would like him to read the message. When Adam sees that he is Cc'd, he thinks, *This isn't to me, I don't need to read it. I'll file it for later.* In this case, Adam will have no idea about the new team priorities. You think Adam is aware of the information and will be ready to support the team, but in reality, he hasn't got a clue what was in the email. This isn't the end of the problem either.

Imagine Julie asks Adam for help with something that is normally her responsibility, and Adam tells her no because he hasn't read the email he was Cc'd on. Then he comes to your office to inform you Julie is passing her work off to others. Not only does Julie not get the help she needs, but Adam is wasting time telling you about a situation that should never have happened. Plus, he looks foolish for complaining about an issue he caused and could have avoided if he had read your email. All this from two different interpretations of what to do when being Cc'd.

If you want to avoid problems with the Cc field when sending an email do one of these two things:

1. Never use the CC field.
2. Explain why somebody is carbon copied.

The simplest way to avoid the problems that come with the Cc field is to not use it. Don't use the Cc line at all and put all the recipients in the To field, which means everybody is going to read it—or at least they won't immediately disregard it.

The alternative to never using the Cc field is to explain why you're using it. If you're sending a message to someone, there's always a purpose for it, and explaining that in your introduction increases the chances that people will take the action you want.

The way to do this is similar to introducing a group email. Simply include a line saying "Everyone in the Cc field, you are getting this message because…"

Be careful though, because even if you do this, you still run the risk of people seeing that they are Cc'd and deciding not to read the email before looking any further to see your instruction and know the purpose that you have for them. This is why option one is the safest option. Don't use the Cc field.

Adding Managers to the Cc

There are two additional reasons people commonly use the Cc field, both involving adding a manager to an email. This might be your own, or the boss of the person you're emailing. The two reasons are:

1. To cover your ass; and/or
2. To apply pressure on the recipient.

Cover Your Ass Emails

Adding a manager to an email happens for many reasons. You might be writing about a contentious topic and want your manager to be aware of the conversation, for example. If you're sending a risky message that's direct or involves a disagreement, the act of copying your manager can provide a feeling of security, like they've got your back. The reasons aren't always negative. Your email might be about a topic the manager is particularly interested in, or you're praising someone and want your manager to see the good work they have done.

Whatever the reason, the rules of Cc'ing still apply. Make sure you explain in the email why you've copied the manager. If you don't, how will they know what you expect or want them to do with the message? Plus, if you've written the subject line and introduction for the benefit of the main recipient, there's a good chance they differ from what you want the manager to do with the email. This means the manager will see an email in their inbox with a topic and purpose meant for someone else and won't know why it's been sent to them.

If you are adding your manager to a conversation to become part of the discussion, follow the approach described later in this section for adding people to group emails.

On the other hand, if you just want your manager to know about a situation, don't copy them, send them a new email about it. That way you can write a meaningful subject line and introduction that is relevant to the topic and purpose you have for the manager.

To Apply Pressure on the Recipient

A common and unfortunate reason for copying a manager on an email is to apply pressure on the recipient. Perhaps someone hasn't replied to you after multiple requests, or they've not sent the document you need. Whatever the reason, you reply to the last message you sent and copy the recipient's manager. This adds pressure on the recipient, saying, "You failed to deliver what I asked for and now your boss knows about it."

This is a passive-aggressive power play. Please don't do it.

If you want someone to reply faster or deliver the thing you need, you should engage with them in real time. Go and see them if you're in the same location, or pick up the phone and talk to them or make a video call. Find out if there is something else they are doing that is a higher priority than what you need. Don't just add their manager and hope you get the outcome you want. There are better ways to handle the situation than copying a manager that will show your professionalism in a much better light.

NOTE: If you'd like a chuckle, check out Steve Burdett's book, *As Per My Previous Email*. It's an amusing look at all the bad habits we have in our work emails and includes an uncannily accurate view into the passive-aggressive ways people use the Cc field.

Team Rules for Cc Are a Trap

Some teams have team rules for how to use Cc in emails.

Perhaps you've agreed with all of the people on your team that if you're copied on an email, the purpose is to read it when you have the time. That's great for the emails you send within your team. But it's less great when you send messages outside your team. If you get familiar with a rule for Cc within your own group, you might forget that people outside your team don't follow those same rules. Anyone outside your team has no idea the rules even exist. They will follow their own team or individual interpretation of the Cc field.

Cc Rules Summary

When sending group messages to anyone, whether inside or outside your team, my advice is don't use the Cc field. And if you do use it, you must make it clear at the start of the email what you intend the Cc'd people to do.

BCC IS NOT FOR SPYING OR SUBTERFUGE

Most email clients give you the option to use a feature called Bcc or Blind Carbon Copy, which is the third field you can use for addressing outgoing email messages.

What is Bcc? It is just like the To and Cc fields, but the difference is that anyone who receives the email will not see any of the recipients listed under Bcc.

Figure 7: The Bcc field is usually under the Cc field but it is not for spying

If I sent an email to you and also Bcc'd three other people, you would only see that the message went to you. You would have no idea that it went to other people as well.

That sounds great, right? You can let people spy on your conversations, like getting a sneak peek into what you're doing.

Wrong!

Blind copy is not a spy feature. It's not designed for you to be able to secretly add people to conversations.

Here are some common uses I've seen for Bcc:

- I'll copy my boss when I send a controversial email message and then the person I'm sending it to won't know my boss is looking.
- I'm confronting someone about a complaint and Bcc'd the accuser so they can see I'm doing something about the incident.
- I want to send a snarky message and thought my colleague would enjoy reading it.
- To hide the contact details of recipients.

The first three reasons are a bit underhanded. It's the equivalent of letting people sneak in and observe a conversation. Not only are they sneaky but the use of Bcc often backfires when a Bcc'd recipient lets slip that they saw the message, and let's face it, the truth usually comes out eventually no matter what.

Think about it this way, would you have a face-to-face conversation with someone while you are wearing a secret microphone for someone else to listen in? Of course you wouldn't. Not only is it rude but in many places recording conversations without everyone involved knowing about it is illegal (unless you're helping the police catch a criminal and they have a warrant).

The fourth reason, which is actually a legitimate use for Bcc, is discussed in more detail a little later in this chapter.

Bcc Creates Extra Work & Mistakes

First, the blind copied recipients don't know why they are getting the email. Throughout this book, you've seen why it's important to tell people the purpose of an email. When you blind copy someone, you can't tell them why they are receiving the email because that would defeat the purpose of blind copying. This means you need to contact them in some other way, by phone, in person, email, etc., to explain why you've copied them on the original email. That's extra work you could avoid by simply forwarding the message to them, where you can explain why they are getting that email forward.

The second issue is that Bcc recipients can still use Reply All. If this is done inadvertently, you can imagine the implications. You copy a colleague on a controversial email, and they accidentally Reply All with some comment about the situation. Their presence is revealed, and their comments are laid bare for all to see. At best, that's embarrassing and unprofessional. At worst, it can cause business deals to fail and trigger disciplinary action.

Both of these are strong reasons for not using the Bcc field. But, if you absolutely must share a message and you don't want the primary recipients to know about it, do this instead:

1. Send the message to the intended recipient; and
2. Then forward a copy of that message to the people you would have Bcc'd.

This way you can explain why they are seeing it and avoid any accidental Reply All mistakes by essentially having two separate conversations on the same topic, one with the main recipient and one with the "secret" person. After all, when the original recipient replies to your message, their reply won't go to the Bcc'd people anyway, so you might as well have two separate emails, each of which is clearly introduced.

The Two Legitimate Uses for Bcc

There are only two legitimate workplace uses for the Blind Carbon Copy function:

1. To protect the names and email addresses of the recipients in a group email; and/or
2. To copy the message to yourself.

If, for example, I was going to send a message to everybody on my company's mailing list, I wouldn't want the email to go out with a thousand different emails and names attached to it. I don't want everybody on the email to get everybody else's information. I want to keep that data secure. Using Bcc for all the recipients helps protect the data of the people you're sending the message to. You'll often find this with newsletters and mailing lists. It can look a little odd because the email is sent to the sender's own address and apparently to no one else. You can't see anyone else's email information, and they can't see yours.

The second legitimate use for Bcc is copying the email to yourself because your filing or follow-up processes need a copy in your inbox. That's not something I do, but I know people who do this and they say it works well for them. If you're wondering what advice I have about doing that, my answer is none. This book isn't about inbox management—it's about writing great emails, so I'll stay clear of advice on that topic.

FORWARDING EMAIL CHAINS

Forwarding an email chain means sending an existing string of emails to a new recipient. It is not a reply, and none of the original conversation participants are included. It is different from adding people to an ongoing email chain, which we cover later in the book. This is about starting a new email conversation by forwarding a long string of existing messages.

If you ever receive forwarded email chains, you might sometimes feel a little bit like this:

Figure 8: Digging through email chains to find the key message is frustrating

You must dig through all the emails in the chain to find out what the conversation is about, what the key information is, and what you're expected to do about it. It's frustrating, right?

If you want to write great emails, don't do this. You don't want to frustrate your recipients by making them read through a long email chain. Instead, take a minute and introduce the email clearly.

Introduce the Chain as a New Email

If you forward an email chain, you should treat it like the beginning of a new conversation. Even though there may be ten or even twenty emails in the chain already, when you send an email chain to a new person, you are starting a new conversation. That means you need to write an introduction just like you would on a brand-new email.

You've got to have a clear subject line and a clear introduction and tell them what the topic is, what the purpose of sending them this email is, and what you're expecting them to do. Plus, of course, any time frames that come with it.

All of the techniques you read about in section one still hold true when you forward an email chain to somebody new.

Change the Subject Line

When starting a new email, the subject line must include a clear topic and purpose. The same is true for a forwarded email chain. This can be tough to remember, especially when the subject line is already populated for you. The subject of the original email chain is in the subject field, often with FW: added in front to indicate the message has been forwarded.

Figure 9: Forwarded emails have pre-populated subject lines - make sure you update it to something meaningful to the recipient

The thing is, this auto-populated subject line might not be the right subject line for your new conversation. The topic may be clear, but the purpose is likely to be incorrect because the purpose of forwarding the message probably isn't the same as the purpose of the original email chain.

When you forward an email chain, or even when you forward a single email, always rewrite the subject line and include the specific purpose you have for the new recipient.

Summarize the Chain

Email chains are long, often disorganized, and are filled with all the header and footer information from each reply. Things like signature lines fill more than 50 percent of the chain. That's a lot of unnecessary and untidy information to scroll through.

You should make it as easy as possible for the recipient to understand what you've sent them. You don't want people to be looking through twenty emails, trying to get a sense of the information.

The easiest way to help the recipient is to summarize the content in the chain. Adding a two or three line summary, giving the key points and the key information from that chain, will help new recipients understand your message. You'll also save them a bunch of time because they won't have to dig through the entire chain to get that information.

This doesn't mean rewriting the entire email chain in your message. All you have to do is pull out the key information, questions, actions, decisions, and any themes in the discussion. The actions might direct the recipient to read a particular portion of the chain, for example, which should be combined with a clear statement of the purpose for them reading it.

Every email chain is different and there is no universal way to summarize them, but a good guide is to think about what you would want to know if the email chain appeared in your inbox. What few things would be really helpful to understand before you read the string of messages? Whatever you would want to know is a decent guide for the minimum that someone else will want to get.

An alternative to copying the content is to highlight key information in the chain. This only works if the content of the chain is well-formatted and logical. It is better than nothing, but I still recommend writing a short summary in your message because that has the greatest chance of being clearly understood.

Never Forward with an FYI

And the last thing I would suggest—actually, not suggest, I beg you not to do this—please never forward an email chain with only the letters "FYI" at the start.

I can't tell you the number of times I've received long email chains that just say "FYI" at the beginning. *What do you want me to do with it? Do you want me to read it? Do you need me to reply? Are there questions buried in the list that I need to answer? Urgh, this is too much effort. I'll read this email later on.* And then it goes into the "read later" folder or slides off the bottom of the screen as my inbox fills with new messages. Either way, the result is the same—it doesn't get read.

When you write the letters "FYI" at the start of a forwarded email, it's not clear to your audience why they are receiving this email chain. So please don't do this. Instead, write a short, clear introduction and a summary of the chain up to that point.

ADDING & REMOVING PEOPLE FROM EMAIL CHAINS

Sometimes during the course of an email chain, you may want to add or remove people from the discussion. When this happens, there are a few rules to follow to make sure that everybody is clear and understands the changes.

1. Tell the group why you've added or removed somebody.
2. Tell the people you add or remove why you've added or removed them.

Adding Someone to an Ongoing Group Email

It doesn't matter if you sent the first email in the chain or you have been included in someone else's email chain, you should always give an explanation when adding new people to the discussion.

If you're in the middle of a group discussion and bring someone else into it, it's polite to let everybody know that a new person has joined. It's also helpful to let the group know why you've invited that new person into the discussion.

Imagine you are in a face-to-face conversation in a group meeting or at a party, then you pull someone else into the group. You'd probably say something like, "Hey, Emma, come and join us. I think you'll find this story interesting." This helps Emma understand why you're asking her to join and tells the group why you've invited Emma to join the discussion.

The same thing is true in a group email. Bringing a new person into the discussion requires an introduction.

To do this, don't just write "+Emma." That isn't fair to Emma because she has to work out why she's been added, as do all the other people in the chain. Instead, write an introduction that does three things:

1. Tells the new additions why they've been added;
2. Tells the group why the new people have been added; and
3. Gives the new addition specific instructions.

It is possible to do all of this in one or two sentences. For example:

> I've invited Emma into the discussion because she has the expertise we need and can help us answer a question.
>
> **Emma**, can you answer the question highlighted below?
>
> *... rest of email chain continues below ...*

If the email chain is long, consider adding a short summary of the discussion to help newcomers understand what they've missed.

Removing Someone from an Ongoing Group Email

The best practices for removing people from email chains are similar to those for adding people. First, explain to the group why these people have been removed. Don't just take people off the distribution list without saying anything. Always include a line in your next reply, informing the group what you've done and why. For example:

> Hey, everyone, I've taken Philip off this email chain because I want to talk about his retirement party surprise.

> Hi, I removed Sarah and Sajid from the chain because they aren't working on this project anymore.

Why is this important? Well, if you reply to an email chain and haven't noticed that somebody has been taken out, you could ask questions or share information aimed at that person. But because they were removed, you won't get an answer. In this situation, the best-case result is that someone else on the email chain tells you the person you want is no longer in the discussion. And the worst case is that you waste days waiting for a reply that will never come, the consequences of which could all have been avoided if it was clearly stated that someone had been taken off the email chain.

If you remove someone from an email chain that isn't yours—meaning you didn't send the first email in the chain—always let the original sender know why you've made that change. They had a reason for adding all the recipients in the beginning, and it's polite to let them know why you've removed someone they had originally included. Ideally, you'd check with them *before* you make the change, but in fast-moving conversations or if someone really shouldn't be part of a conversation, that isn't always possible. You may need to make the change and then follow up with the original sender.

In addition to explaining to the group, you should also send a note to the people who have been removed. They won't know they've been removed unless someone tells them. If you're receiving an email chain and then the messages stop arriving, you might think the conversation has ended but not know why.

Sending a note to the people you've removed is simple. For example:

Hi Aaron,

I've taken you off this email chain because we've finished talking about your section and I don't want to fill your inbox with emails about topics you're not impacted by.

If you have any questions about this, let me know.

Thanks,
Chris

Whatever the reason is, as long as it's a good and valid reason, let people know that you've removed them and why.

Doing this also gives them the opportunity to say, "No, I'd like to come back in, please." They may have a reason to be included that you're not aware of.

The key thing here is to always be open about changes. If you remove people or add people without being open about it, it's impolite. It's also not helpful for the people who are being added or removed, and it's not helpful for the group.

The exception to this is if you've removed someone and deliberately don't want them to know. Examples include removing a customer to continue the conversation with internal staff only, or removing Steve from the chain because you're discussing his next pay raise. In some situations, it makes sense not to tell people when they've been removed from a chain, but most of the time it's best to let people know.

When Other People Change the Recipients on Your Email Chain

It's not uncommon to start a group email and then, later in the discussion, notice that someone has added or removed recipients from the chain. If this happens, and they have explained the reason for the change in their email, and you agree with it, then it's fine. You can accept the changes and carry on.

An alternative scenario is when they make a change and it is not explained. In this case, the next step is not to reverse the change in your next message. Don't immediately add the people back in or remove unexpected additions. Instead, take a moment and ask why they did it, preferably with a phone call or instant message rather than by replying to the whole group in the email. If after speaking to them, you find you agree with the reason, you can leave the changes as they are. Perhaps you could use the opportunity to show them the benefits of writing an explanation in the email where they've made the change. Even better, give them a copy of this book!

If the result of the conversation is that you don't agree with the change of recipients, you need to decide how to handle it with the person who made the change. You both have reasons for including or removing specific participants and it's unlikely those reasons will clash. Usually, a quick discussion is enough to resolve any issues. When you've come to an agreement, you can continue or reverse the changes (whichever is appropriate) in the next message.

KEEPING AN EMAIL CHAIN FOCUSED

Sometimes email chain discussions can get a little unfocused. They drift away from the original topic, replies are sent out of order, multiple answers appear for the same question, and so on.

The two most common problems in long email chains are confusion about the topic, and topic drift.

Confusion About the Topic

If there's an email discussion involving five, ten, or more participants, different people will send replies at different times. Unlike a face-to-face conversation where body language and verbal cues tell us who has an answer and wants to speak next, email has none of that. Not only do we not have the visual cues but recipients will see the email at different times, some immediately after it is sent and others may not see it until the next day.

This asynchronous communication style leads to the following situations:

- Multiple people reply at the same time but to different pieces of the previous message.
- Two people give different answers to the same question.
- Replies can often come out of sequence.
- Somebody replies to an earlier message, not realizing there's a more recent one in the discussion.

You can see how easily things become confused. In these situations, it is best to stop the email chain and arrange a phone call or meeting so that the conversation can be more organized.

If you recognize that there's confusion, you should reset the email chain with a summary. In your next reply, say something like:

> I think we may have lost track of the thread. We may be getting some things out of order. I'd just like to summarize where we are at the moment to bring us all back to the same place.

Then you can summarize the original purpose, what's been discussed so far, key decisions that have been made, the next steps and/or any remaining open questions, and so on.

A short summary will help get everybody back to the same place and alleviate any confusion. After a summary, everyone in the group gets to start again from the same common understanding.

Topic Drift

In a group discussion, much like a face-to-face discussion, conversations can move away from the original topic as new ideas come in. Someone points out how the original topic relates to a new topic, and the conversation shifts to talk about the new topic.

The problems this causes are:

- The subject and purpose of the topic no longer match the subject line.
- Filing and organizing emails becomes harder because multiple topics share the same subject.
- The new topic might not be relevant to the original recipients, but they still get the emails.

The solution to topic drift is similar to solving email chain confusion. Just reset the conversation with a summary. Reply to the group with a statement about the topic drifting away from the original purpose. Include a short summary reminding people of the original intent and a couple of lines about where you are in completing the original purpose of the group email. Then say what you think should happen next.

For example:

> Hey folks, I think we've moved away from our original intent.
>
> The original purpose of this chain was to answer five questions about next week's client meeting. We are almost done, we've got answers to three of the five questions.
>
> Can we answer these two remaining questions and then we can move on to the new topic Steve raised about the client project?

Resetting with a summary refocuses the chain and everybody then gets more value out of the rest of that discussion.

When is an Email Chain Too Long?

There is no limit on how long an email chain can go on. What does matter is that it stays focused and on topic. If the discussion gets confused or the topic changes, the chain should be reset. If the reset doesn't work, the discussion should change to a new channel (phone call, meeting, etc.).

Likewise, if the original purpose of the email has been achieved, the email chain should end. Any new topics should be addressed in a separate email chain.

CHANGING TOPICS IN AN EMAIL CHAIN

Email chains may start out with one topic, but at some point during the back and forth, they can move on to a new or different topic. When this happens, stop. You shouldn't change the topic in an email thread.

Why? Because it can confuse and frustrate the recipients. The new topic will not match the original topic and purpose of the discussion. Back in section one when you read about three types of email to avoid, one was bait and switch. When you change the topic of an email, it can feel like a bait and switch for the reader. Plus, it is a pain to file and organize the messages.

If there is a change in the original purpose of the email, it will be due to one of these causes:

1. A deliberate change; or
2. An unintentional change.

In each case, there are a few simple things you can do to keep the communication flowing without confusion.

A Deliberate Change of Topic

A deliberate change in the topic in a group email happens when the original purpose has been accomplished and the conversation changes to some new topic or purpose. Unfortunately, changing topics in an existing email chain causes a few problems.

1. The subject line is still related to the original topic and purpose of the email.
2. The group of people who were put together for the original purpose might not be the right group for the new purpose.
3. People filing emails by subject won't see the separation between the two topics.
4. People may ignore future emails because they believe the original topic is complete and the new emails with the same subject are unnecessary chatter.

To avoid these problems, and any others you might think of, don't change topics in an email thread. Instead, when you want to deliberately change the topic, close the old email chain, wrap it up with a summary, and then start a new one. In the summary, you can say the new topic will be covered in a new chain with the appropriate people, which makes it clear that the conversation is complete and helps the new topic get a good start. A good start that comes with a clear topic, purpose, and introduction.

The steps to do this are simple:

1. Don't start a new topic in the old thread.
2. Open a new email.
3. Write a clear subject line and introduction.
4. Add the people you need.
5. Hit Send.

Anyone who tracks the conversation using the subject line in their email folders won't get the topics mixed up, there's less chance of including people you don't need in the new topic, and all the recipients can file the emails however they want.

An Unintentional Change of Topic

We touched on the unintentional topic change earlier, when a topic drifts away from the original purpose. Another cause of this change is when somebody asks a question that's tangential to the original conversation. In this case, the conversation takes a turn and goes off to that new topic. Neither of these is a deliberate change. They just happen sometimes in the normal flow of a discussion.

When unintentional changes happen, you should stop it as soon as possible. Reset the email chain and then split the two topics into separate email threads.

Step 1: Reset the email chain.

As described earlier in this section, you can reset the chain by writing a summary. Highlight the fact that the conversation has moved away from the original purpose and direct the discussion back to that purpose.

Example:

> "Hi folks, I think we've moved away from the original goal of this email chain. We started talking about Topic ABC and are now talking about topic 123. Please can we finish Topic ABC first before moving on to something new?"

This should be enough to bring the discussion back to the original topic and purpose.

Step 2: Start a separate email for the new topic.

An alternative, which works well when the new conversation is valid and worthwhile, is to start a new email. In this case, you can reply to the ongoing email chain and tell them you'll start a new email chain on the second topic.

Example:

> "Hi folks, we have got two topics of conversation in this email. I'm going to start a new email chain on topic number two so we can continue topic number one in this chain with the current subject line, etc. The new email subject line will be about Topic 2."

In most cases, you'll need to do both steps. The original topic will need to be complete and you probably don't want to ignore the new topic. Get your original email chain back on track and set up a new email so you can address both topics in two separate conversation threads.

WHEN THE CONVERSATION MOVES BEYOND EMAIL

There are times when a group email conversation moves beyond email. It may turn into a meeting or a face-to-face conversation, or you might contact someone via instant message to discuss the topic.

Whatever the new method of communication, when the conversation moves beyond email, be aware of:

- Introducing parallel conversations; and
- Excluding people.

Imagine you and I are part of a group email with five other recipients, and after a few emails have been sent, I call you to discuss the topic. The moment I talk to you, the rest of the group has been left out.

Sure, it's great that we've made progress and I'm all for changing the communication channel if it helps make progress, but this type of change in a group email causes a communication problem. The rest of the group, the people who weren't in on our one-to-one conversation, won't be aware of what happened. We've cut them out of the loop. This multi-channel communication causes people within the group to become misaligned and leads to confusion and frustration.

Not only that, but if the email chain continues while we have our conversation on the phone, we're faced with a split conversation—two parallel lines of communication with different inputs, different decision-making, and different progress. At some point, the two lines of communication need to merge back together.

There are two ways to handle this situation, depending on urgency and advance scheduling needs:

1. Let the group know you are going to have a call/meeting and will then report back to the group on the outcome of the conversation.
2. Have the conversation and immediately report back to the group.

In both cases, the group is made aware of the separate communication and informed of the outcome. If you communicate with someone by instant message, phone, or meeting, come back to the email chain and inform the whole group of what was done and decided. You don't need to give a blow-by-blow description of the conversation. But if you'd had a discussion with someone and made a decision, inform the whole group that a decision was made.

> "Hi everyone, I spoke with Sanjeet and we agreed we're going to use option three, and here's why..."

Whenever you choose to change the communication method from group email to something else, it's important to close the loop. Return to the email chain and update everyone on what happened outside the email conversation.

Email to Meeting Then Back to Email Again

Sometimes it makes sense to turn an email chain into a meeting or group phone call. This can help if the email has gone on for a while, is getting confusing, or isn't the right format for the discussion anymore.

If the meeting includes all the email recipients, no one is left out and everyone remains in sync. But if you only have part of the group in the meeting, anyone who's not part of it isn't going to follow along with the discussion. To avoid this issue, there's one simple thing you can do. Inform the whole group there will be a meeting and then what the outcome of the meeting was.

Does this update have to be by email? Not always. If the group is together in the same location, a verbal update might be okay. But if the group is not all together, you should send the update by email. I suggest replying to the last message in the original email chain and summarizing what happened in the meeting. The specific situation, topic, and purpose will determine if the conversation then continues by email, ends, or is moved to a new email chain. Whatever you choose, always come back and inform the group what happened.

It sounds simple, but you'd be surprised how often it doesn't happen.

ASSESSMENT: WHAT ARE THE BEST PRACTICES FOR GROUP AND CHAIN EMAILS?

The questions in this test will show how many of the tips and methods you can recall from the training so far. Each question is multiple choice, and the answers are available at the end.

1. What should be in the introduction of a group email?
    A. The topic
    B. Detailed information and background
    C. The purpose of the email
    D. Explanation of why the group or subgroups are receiving the email
    E. A list of actions

2. What are the standard rules for adding people to the Cc line?

    A. People Cc'd don't need to take any action
    B. People Cc'd must read the email
    C. People Cc'd can take as long as they want to read and reply
    D. People Cc'd must not reply; they are there only to observe the conversation
    E. There are no standard rules; everyone treats Cc differently

3. When is it appropriate to include people in the Bcc line?

    A. When you want your boss to see a reply
    B. To keep the names and emails of all recipients secure
    C. To let colleagues secretly observe a conversation
    D. To send a copy of the message to yourself
    E. Never use Bcc, it's just for people who want to be sneaky

4. What are some good practices when forwarding an email chain to someone new?

   A. Just write "FYI" to keep the email short
   B. Say why you are sending it to them
   C. Summarize the email chain
   D. Say what action or response is needed
   E. Tell everyone in the original email that you've forwarded the chain

5. What should you do when adding new people to an existing email chain?

   A. Include a line to tell the new additions why you added them
   B. Continue the conversation without doing anything different
   C. Tell the group that you've added people, name the people and say why
   D. Tell the group you've added people but don't waste time with the details
   E. Summarize the email chain up to that point for the benefit of the new additions

6. What should you do when removing people from an email chain?

   A. Continue the conversation without doing anything different
   B. Include a line to tell the group you've removed people but don't waste time with the details
   C. Include a line in the next email to tell the remaining people that you've removed people, name the people/ group and say why

7. Should you send a message to people you've removed from an email chain?

   A. Yes
   B. No
   C. It depends on the situation

8. How can you refocus an email chain that is confusing or has drifted away from the original purpose?

   A. Stop emailing and set up a phone call or meeting
   B. Summarize the conversation to refocus the group
   C. Remove people from the chain to have fewer opinions

9. What is a good way to start a new topic in an existing email chain?

   A. Change the subject line in your next reply
   B. Start talking about the new topic in your next reply
   C. Don't. Instead, start a new email chain for the new topic and include a clear introduction

Answers are on the next page

ANSWERS

1. A, C, D
2. E
3. B, D
4. B, C, D (E is optional)
5. A, C, (E is optional)
6. C
7. C
8. B (A is optional)
9. C

You can download a copy of this assessment here:
https://chrisfenning.com/resources/

SECTION 4 :
OTHER TIPS & ADVICE

In the course of writing this book, I received questions that didn't fit into the three previous sections. Rather than ignore them, I've included them in this final part of the book. Some of the questions would need entire books to give a complete answer while others only need a few lines. In each case, I've shared my thoughts and advice as briefly as possible, and in some cases, you'll also find links to other resources that can help.

If you have a question about work emails that isn't in this section or answered elsewhere in this book, you can send it to me at chris@chrisfenning.com. I will do my best to answer your question and perhaps even add it to a future version of this book.

For now, these are the questions covered in the next few pages:

- What should go into an out-of-office auto-reply?
- Are there any tips for managing an overloaded email inbox?
- Are there any rules about using acronyms in email?
- How important are spelling and grammar?
- When writing in a non-native language are there extra rules to follow?
- Are work emails private?
- Can I effectively manage negative exchanges by email?
- If an email chain turns into a debate should it become a meeting?
- How do I know if I send too many emails?
- Does my tone of voice come across in an email?
- Is it OK to use emojis in an email?
- How do cultural considerations impact emails?
- What should I put in my signature block?
- Does it matter how I sign off my emails?

WHAT SHOULD GO INTO AN OUT-OF-OFFICE AUTO-REPLY?

If you want to know when to use an out-of-office reply, check what your company and team expect. Everywhere is different, and the best source of guidance comes from the people around you.

As for what to write in your out-of-office message, there are three things you should do:

1. Provide information people need;
2. Keep it short and informative; and
3. Never leave it blank.

At the very least, your out-of-office message should say how long you will be away and give specific dates. For example, "I am away from work for a week starting on Monday, the 15th of March. I'll be back in the office on Monday, the 22nd of March." If you say, "I'm out from the 15th to the 19th of March," people might think you will respond on the 19th without realizing there is a weekend. Be completely clear and state the day you will be back to work.

If you have arranged for other people to cover for you during your time way, you can list them in the message. For example, "For questions about reports, talk to Jeff. For anything connected to Project Everest, talk to Sandra. For anything else, I'll reply when I get back." This helps people know if an alternative contact is available and who to contact. Make sure you only list people you've spoken to and agreed will provide cover. Otherwise, they will be surprised and you won't be very popular when you get back.

Finally, if you want to add personal topics to the message, for instance saying where you are going and what you're doing, that's up to you and the culture of the organization you work for. See what the people around you do and do what feels right for you.

ARE THERE ANY TIPS FOR MANAGING AN OVERLOADED EMAIL INBOX?

If you write clear emails using the advice in this book, you should get fewer replies that are also of higher quality. That by itself will help reduce the number of emails in your inbox.

Beyond that, there are many ways to manage an email inbox, and each person has different preferences, which makes this topic outside the scope of this book. If you'd like specific tips or advice, a quick search online will give you hundreds of articles with advice.

Alternatively, you can check out this curated list of email management advice from the Harvard Business Review at https://hbr.org/2021/11/managing-your-inbox-our-favorite-reads

ARE THERE ANY RULES ABOUT USING ACRONYMS IN EMAIL?

The same rules for acronyms apply to email as they do to any other communication. Never assume recipients will know what it means but rather always explain the acronym when you use it first. Simply spelling it out and putting the acronym in parentheses once is typically enough.

My personal preference is to not use acronyms at all. Many of the acronyms and initialisms we use only have meaning to people with our jobs or skillset. Avoid using them. Instead, describe whatever you are talking about using general terms that email recipients will understand. For example, instead of saying, "The ComDat system," say, "The customer information database." This language is clear and everyone will understand it.

How important are spelling and grammar?

Spelling and grammar are important in emails. The exact standard for accuracy in emails will depend on where you work and who you are writing to.

Sending an email to an important external client requires a higher standard of accuracy than asking your colleague what they want for lunch. Keep in mind that in both cases, accuracy is better. Repeated errors, even to close friends and colleagues, will show other people you lack attention to detail.

Another factor in the importance of spelling and grammar is if you're writing in your native language. When writing in a language that you are not fluent in, there is greater tolerance for mistakes. See the next question for more on this topic.

When writing in a non-native language are there extra rules to follow?

When writing in a language that you are not fluent in, keep the wording in your emails simple. Short sentences with common words are much more likely to be understood than complex sentences with multiple clauses. Short sentences are also more likely to be grammatically correct. By the way, this is the same advice I give to native speakers. Short, simple sentences are easier to understand.

If you are worried about grammar mistakes or sounding too direct, include a note saying you are "writing in a non-native language and hope the message doesn't seem abrupt or rude." When working in a multinational environment, it is easy to forget that the people around us might not speak our language fluently. A little reminder of that helps us be more understanding.

ARE WORK EMAILS PRIVATE?

Something you may not consider but should be aware of, is your work emails are not private. Anything you send at work can be used in legal proceedings by or against the company you work for, though they can even be used against you directly.

Now, it's unlikely that your email to Dave in sales to check a price will ever be needed in court. But you don't know what can happen in the future. Avoid including anything that would be embarrassing to you or the company in the future and keep all your work emails strictly professional.

Be especially careful when writing about other people. An HR complaint could result in a review of emails to support an accusation of bullying, harassment, or other inappropriate behavior. If you never write anything bad, mean, or offensive about other people, you won't have any issues. A good principle to follow is to never write anything you wouldn't be okay with having read out loud in court, or to your mother. Polite and professional is the best approach.

CAN I EFFECTIVELY MANAGE NEGATIVE EXCHANGES BY EMAIL?

A question I'm often asked is, "How should we handle conflict in email?" My advice is don't use email for this. Any contentious topics or topics that are likely to cause negative reactions should always be delivered in person.

It may feel easier to write an email, but there is no verbal or physical feedback, so you can't see how the recipient is reacting to the message. That means you can't alter the message to make the meaning clear.

Instead of writing an email, pick up the phone or arrange to speak to them in person. It might be less comfortable, but you will avoid issues caused by the misinterpretation of an email.

IF AN EMAIL CHAIN TURNS INTO A DEBATE, SHOULD IT BECOME A MEETING?

It's not uncommon to have long email chains turn into debates. It could be a difference of opinion about which option to choose, or two people describing events from different perspectives. Whatever the situation, when an email chain becomes a debate, the conversation needs to change to a different medium.

Exactly which method to use will depend on the location and availability of the people involved. Either meet face-to-face, get on a video call, or speak on the phone. It may help to have a small group discussion with the few people who are actively debating each other rather than bring all the email recipients together.

When the debate issue is resolved it may be possible to continue the email chain, or you may need to end it and continue the communication in another format or a new email chain.

HOW DO I KNOW IF I SEND TOO MANY EMAILS?

Writing great emails is a good way to make every message relevant and short. But what do you do if you think you are sending too many emails?

The simplest thing to do is to ask the people you send emails to. Pick up the phone or go and see them. Tell them you want to know if your communication is working well, then ask if you send too many emails. You can use the opportunity to ask if they would prefer a different type of communication for specific messages. This conversation will give you all you need to adapt to the style they like while telling you if you are sending too many messages.

Another approach is to review the emails you send before talking to other people. The "Am I sending too many emails?" test will help:

The "*Am I sending too many emails?*" Test

Look at your sent emails and find the person you send the most emails to. Using a filter in your email application should make this easy. Then follow these four steps:

Step 1: Look for emails with similar topics sent on the same day.

Ask yourself, "Could this have been included in the other emails I sent on a similar topic?"

If yes, you're probably sending too many emails and should either combine some or pick up the phone to have a conversation about all the topics in one go. Review section one for more advice on handling multiple topics in emails.

Step 2: Look for really short emails (e.g., single-question or single-line updates).

Ask yourself these questions:

- Could this have been sent by instant message, Slack, or over the phone?
- Could these have been combined into a single multi-topic email?

If yes, try and use the alternative method of communication next time.

Step 3: Contact the person.

The next step is to contact the person you sent the emails to using a non-email method like instant message, phone, in-person, etc. Ask them how they would like to get messages from you.

Steps 1 and 2 will have helped you prepare for the conversation. You'll have an idea of the number and type of messages you could have sent by a different method or combined into a single email.

You can ask specific questions about how they like to receive short messages versus longer ones and if messages on a similar topic should be grouped into a single email. You'll only know if you ask.

Whatever they tell you, you will know if you are sending the right number of emails or if you are sending too many. If they like email, they might tell you to keep doing what you're doing. If they prefer something else, they will tell you and you can change what you do to help them. Either way, they will be grateful to you for asking.

Step 4: Repeat the process.

After you've spoken to the person you email most, repeat this process for the next person you send a lot of emails to. You'll be addressing the biggest volume first, and if you get consistent replies about how to communicate short messages, you can start to apply those changes to the other people you send emails to.

This process takes time, so don't expect to do it all in a day. Try contacting one person a week until you've spoken to your most frequent contacts. It is a thoughtful thing to do, and your colleagues will appreciate the effort you make to understand their email and general communication preferences.

DOES MY TONE OF VOICE COME ACROSS IN AN EMAIL?

Every email has a tone of voice, but it isn't necessarily the tone you intended. The way we read messages is affected by many things. Our current mood, what we think about the person sending it, recent experience, and more. It is possible for two people to read the same message in two different ways.

A friend told me a story about sending an email to a colleague and her boss about handing over some work. The boss came to see her and said, "You should write an apology. That was quite demanding and not a nice email to send." A moment later the phone rang. It was the colleague calling to say thanks for such a great idea and to arrange a time to hand over the work. The exact same message was interpreted in two very different ways.

You never know how someone will read and interpret your emails, and no matter what you write, it can be misinterpreted. You can try this for yourself. Find a recent email someone has sent you. Read it in a happy voice—think about unicorns and kittens. Then read it in an angry voice—think about rush hour traffic. Then imagine the person was being sarcastic. Does the meaning of the message stay the same each time? Or do you interpret the message differently? I bet you find some differences each time.

The lack of tone of voice and visual signals like body language makes it easier for us to put our own spin on any message we read.

What does this mean for your emails? It means you should be careful about what you write. At the same time, we shouldn't overthink things. No matter how careful we are, there is always a way for our words to be misinterpreted.

The advice given earlier about negative exchanges helps here. The more contentious, unwelcome, or impactful the topic, the more important it is to communicate in person.

One way to reduce the risk of misinterpretation is to include labels to show when you're joking or being sarcastic. A couple of words in parenthesis like (I'm joking!) can help recipients understand when you are being serious and when you are joking.

If you are writing about a "delicate" topic or something that may involve some strong feelings, pause between writing and sending the message. Finish writing the email, but don't send it. Step away, either physically or mentally, and review what you've written at a later time. Even a few minutes' gap can help you see if the message has the feel or tone you want to convey. You can also get a friend or colleague to read the message before you send it. A second set of eyes may see a different tone than the one you intended.

Is it ok to use emojis in an email?

Another way to make your tone clearer is to use emoticons (emojis), and they are becoming increasingly common in emails. Most forms of electronic communication include some form of emoji. Some email clients even make it easy to add them by converting punctuation into smiley faces for you.

Some people frown on the use of emojis in emails. Other people find it almost impossible not to use them. Once again, the situation you are in will determine what is appropriate. Formal emails to a client informing them about a legal case probably shouldn't include any emojis. But a message to your team about a recent success could be full of them. The culture of your team, company, and your own style, coupled with the purpose and formality of the message should determine what is appropriate to use.

How do cultural considerations impact emails?

Personality and culture play an important part in how we communicate. Some people and cultures like to communicate directly and get straight to the point. Others are more circumspect and include layers of nuance in the meaning of their messages.

Erin Meyer has described these differences brilliantly in her book, *The Culture Map: Breaking Through the Invisible Boundaries of Global Business.* If you work in a culturally diverse environment, I highly recommend reading her book, especially chapter 1, which focuses on the communication style differences between countries.

While there are significant differences in the way cultures communicate, the fundamental components of the methods described throughout this book do not change. Every recipient needs to get the key information early in an email—what the message is about, what they should do with it, time frames, and so on. These things are necessary for a clear understanding of a message regardless of anything else. What can change between countries and cultures is the style and number of words used to communicate each piece of information.

For example, in some countries, it is perfectly acceptable to write, "Please send me your answers by the end of the day." In another country, that may be seen as too direct and would be worded differently, like, "I appreciate your help and quick response." Some readers may interpret this second message as meaning the same thing as the first and send a reply before the end of the day.

I cannot begin to explain the variations in cultural communication around the entire world, but, as mentioned before, if you'd like to understand this topic better, Erin Meyer has done a great job in her book. What I will say here is that if you feel any of the advice in this book conflicts with your normal cultural communication style, particularly if the examples feel too direct, use the frameworks and methods but adapt the words you use to deliver the meaning you need.

WHAT SHOULD I PUT IN MY SIGNATURE BLOCK?

Signatures aren't something you need to spend lots of time on. As long as it is clear, contains the info you think is important, and meets your company criteria, then it does the job. Do you want to add a quote or a funny statement to add some personality? Go right ahead. As long as it isn't inappropriate and doesn't get you in trouble at work there is no harm.

Here's how I experience email signatures:

If the emails are clear and well-written, a plain signature doesn't even register and a funny signature may cause me to smile. But if the emails are unclear and difficult to understand, an over-the-top signature gives the impression that the sender isn't very professional. If your signature stands out, you need to be sure your emails are valuable.

This is just my opinion, and yours may be different. I'm not in a position to say who among us is right or wrong. What I can say is that the signature block is much less important than the subject line, introduction, and content of the email. Get those things right and you'll have a lot more freedom to personalize your signature without people getting all judgy.

DOES IT MATTER HOW I SIGN OFF MY EMAILS?

It seems fitting to end the book with a few words about email sign offs. Earlier in the book, I talked about greetings and how they are much less important than people think. The same is true for how you sign off an email. The way you sign off isn't nearly as important as the clarity and brevity of the main message.

The appropriateness of a sign off depends on your culture, the company culture where you work, how well you know the person you're emailing, the formality of the message, what the people around you use, and much, much more. Not only that, but specific sign off styles go in and out of fashion over the years.

I'm not giving you any advice about the specific sign off to use or not use because I don't believe there are any universal rules for the right or wrong way to do it. If your message has been clear, to the point, and delivered what the recipient needs, who cares if you end with best, regards, best regards, thanks, or something else? Does it really matter?

Okay, I admit there are some boundaries. For example, I wouldn't swear or be rude. But that really should be obvious.

Just like choosing your greeting, you need to work out what sign off is best based on the situation you are in. If you're really unsure what to use, look at what the people you work with do. Are your colleagues formal or not? Are customer emails ended in the same way as internal emails? A quick look at other emails in your company will give you much better guidance than I can.

And finally, this is worth repeating, nothing is more important than the quality and clarity of the content in your emails. Write clear, concise messages, and people won't care how you sign off at the end.

EFFECTIVE EMAILS

RESOURCES

To help you apply the methods from this book, you can download the summaries, tips, activities, and assessments for free on my website at https://chrisfenning.com/resources/

This is a list of the resources you can download:

- Quick tips list
- All the checklists and activities in this book
- All the tests and self-assessments in this book
- All the section summaries
- Blog posts about other aspects of email at work

If you'd like to make it even easier to remember and apply what you've learned, get this content delivered to you via the BrainBump™ App.

Follow the instructions below to get started:

1. Visit https://brainbumpapp.com
2. Download the app to your phone
3. Scan the QR code below using the app (not your phone camera)
4. Enjoy faster, easier learning

QUICK TIPS

If you're looking for a condensed version of the advice in this book, here are the main tips for writing effective emails:

The First Few Lines

1. Put the topic in the subject line.
2. Make the purpose clear in the subject line.
3. Indicate urgency in the subject line if appropriate.
4. Say what you need in the first line.
5. Say when you need a response.
6. Deliver your key message in the first lines.
7. Summarize key information.
8. Say if you have multiple topics and how many.
9. State how many questions you've asked in the email.
10. Only change a subject line in a reply if there is an error.
11. Don't say thank you at the start of an email.
12. Don't worry about which greeting to use.

Length, Layout & Formatting

1. Write short emails—they are more likely to be read.
2. Use short paragraphs and bullet points.
3. Put questions, actions, and decisions on their own lines.
4. Label questions, actions, and decisions.
5. Write actions using the format "*who* will do *what* by *when.*"
6. Requests should say who will do what by when.
7. Write decisions using the format "*who* decided *what* and *when.*"
8. Repeat the questions from other people's emails when answering them in yours.
9. Longer emails need more structure.

10. Multi-topic emails need more structure.
11. Use attachments and links to keep supplemental detail out of the email.
12. Use clickable hyperlinks instead of text URLs.
13. Use templates for recurring emails.

Group Emails, Email Chains, & Forwarding

1. If you must use Cc, explain why.
2. Don't use Bcc for spying.
3. Only use Bcc for keeping data secure or sending a copy to yourself.
4. Explain to the group why you added someone to an email chain.
5. Tell someone why you added them to a group email.
6. Explain to the group why you removed someone from an email chain.
7. Tell someone why you removed them from a group email.
8. Add a summary when forwarding an email chain.
9. Never introduce a forwarded email chain with "FYI."
10. Refocus an email chain that's drifted by reminding the group of the original intent.
11. Don't change topics in an email chain. Instead, start a new chain for the new topic.
12. If a conversation moves beyond email, come back to the email chain to summarize what happened.

END NOTES

1. Stephen Monsell, "Task Switching. Trends in Cognitive Sciences." Scientific Research, March 2003. Vol 7, Iss 3, Pgs 134-140. http://dx.doi.org/10.1016/S1364-6613(03)00028-7
2. "Clickbait." Merriam-Webster.com Dictionary. https://www.merriam-webster.com/dictionary/clickbait
3. Wikipedia contributors, "Clickbait." Wikipedia, The Free Encyclopedia. https://en.wikipedia.org/w/index.php?title=Clickbait&oldid=1110875297
4. "Bait and switch." Merriam-Webster.com Dictionary. https://www.merriam-webster.com/dictionary/bait%20and%20switch
5. Chris Fenning, The First Minute: How to Start Conversations That Get Results. Alignment Group Ltd, November 13, 2020.
6. Laura M. Giurge, Vanessa K. Bohns, "You don't need to answer right away! Receivers overestimate how quickly senders expect responses to non-urgent work emails." Organizational Behavior and Human Decision Processes, 2021. Vol 167, Pgs 114-128, ISSN 0749-5978. https://doi.org/10.1016/j.obhdp.2021.08.002 https://www.sciencedirect.com/science/article/abs/pii/S0749597821000807
7. Drs Todd Rogers and Jessica Lasky-Fink, "Write shorter messages. Research confirms: Simpler communications are much more likely to be read." https://www.bostonglobe.com/2020/12/19/opinion/write-shorter-messages/
8. https://quoteinvestigator.com/2012/04/28/shorter-letter/

9. Steven Macdonald, "The Science Behind Email Open Rates (And How to Get More People to Read Your Emails)." SuperOffice, 2022. https://www.superoffice. com/blog/email-open-rates/

10. Ana Gajić, "Mobile Email Statistics." 99Firms. https:// 99firms.com/blog/mobile-email-statistics/#gref

11. James P Van Overschelde, Alice F Healy, "A blank look in reading: the effect of blank space on the identification of letters and words during reading." Exp Psychol, 2005. 52(3):213-23. doi: 10.1027/1618-3169.52.3.213. PMID: 16076069.

12. Presentation by Dennis Hill, IT manager at Crescent Electric, Alex Panagides, CEO at mxHero, and Mike Silano, solution architect at Box. Entitled Archive Emails and Banish Attachments with Box + mxHero"

13. The Radicati Group, Inc., "Email statistics report 2021 – 2025." (2021)

14. Merriam-Webster, "On the History of 'Cc' and 'Bcc'." https://www.merriam-webster.com/words-at-play/ meaning-history-cc-and-bcc-email.

ACKNOWLEDGMENTS

This book wouldn't have been possible without the help, support, and input of some amazing people.

Danielle, once again, you've given me two of the most valuable gifts an author can receive—the time to write and the belief that I can create something helpful. Your love and support made this book possible. Thank you.

Debra L. Hartmann, thank you for taking my words and molding them into something readable. Everyone who reads this book will benefit from your attention to detail and the way you make the reader's experience seamless. I look forward to working together on many more books in the future.

Hassan Osman, your book, *Don't Reply All*, is fantastic. I enjoy your writing and am so grateful you allowed me to include one of your tips in this book. Even having written this book, I continue to recommend *Don't Reply All* to people looking for advice about writing great work emails.

A huge thank you must go to the generous people who reviewed the early drafts. Your ideas, suggestions, and tactful critiques ultimately shaped this book. Whole sections were added and others rearranged based on your feedback. Everyone who reads this book should be grateful to you: David James, SD Shantinath, Harsha Boralessa, Alex Shand, Heather Torretta, Shanna Rone, Yasmina Khelifi, David Sims, Luke Grimstrup, Dikesh Shah, Johnny Ball, Diane Bergman, and Colin Kendall. Thank you.

Lastly, I want to thank all the people who put up with the thousands of bad emails I've sent throughout my career. Thank you for replying and for showing me how to do it better. Many of your good examples have inspired the advice in this book.

To all of you who've read this far, it's time for me to stop writing.

Thanks, best, regards, best regards, all the best, yours sincerely, bye for now…

Chris

<u>Your free book is waiting</u>

Whether you are heading towards senior leadership, are in the middle of your career, or are a recent graduate, this workbook will help you build the critical skill of clear and concise communication at work

Get a free copy of *The First Minute Workbook* here:
https://chrisfenning.com/get-the-first-minute-workbook-free/
(normally $30)

Printed in Great Britain
by Amazon

49208465R00089